Random Notes on Paradise

Note book 1

A man made paradise will soon be practical by proper
drugs or progress. A utopian paradise could still progress.
Quality and its synonyms would be in pleasure. There is
no stress to relieve. There is just pleasure during any ill
health. Ones dreams are more often fulfilled. There is a
more positive kind of health and I don't mean perfect
fitness. Inspiration is more frequent, thinking positive.
Naturalness is there. Harmony is there, satisfaction and
pleasure exists instead of a wealth emphasis. Cost benefit
analysis is still in use. There is self-esteem. Excellence is
growing, wellbeing is high in feeling. There is help to find
friends and affection. A total value is the average value
times the number of cases. Have the most good in
paradise and naturalness and right. Paradise will best
serve the great subjects. Be so great in meaning or an
alternative to meaning that there is nothing greater. If
good progresses better than bad it will gain more
considerations in its favour than bad and serve the
greater subjects. But there is an infinite number of steps
superseding greatness and meaning, and a no maximum
in subjects. The infinites in a way are no maximums. The
subjects make their entities partly existing by aspects of
their nature. Work one wouldn't want to do is
automated. Inner powers are liberated. Special moments
are more special. Happiness lasts. Beauty has power.
Each moment is a treasure well worthwhile. The heart
matters. Sentimental is not a wrong word. Progress is

1

quicker. The arts are heightened. Exaltation can be
heightened by appreciation. There is effortless living,
beautiful gardens, attraction. Drugs without bad.
Humour. Taking your time. There is high normalness, a
military with weapons that don't hurt and don't kill.
Quality focussed, and higher pleasures. Nature works like
the reason. It has mathematics for example, and can be
understood. This is halfway to quality and has slight
quality. Skill is halfway to quality. Quality is a special
branch of knowledge, a treasure with advantages. The
more advantages the more quality. Knowledge is
appropriate to interest. Interest adds quality and
incentive to knowledge. The order in nature is part way
to quality. Evolution creates quality. Some complexity
creates quality in the brain for example, or the computer.
Good raises the richness of emotion and gives us
meaning. Bad discourages itself, and has disadvantages.
Truth and the worthwhile are not synonyms. Truth
contains the worthwhile as a subject and it gives the truth
point and light. Making life work means giving it enough
worthwhileness. Infinity quality may be added to the
search for better or further, even if that means a loss of
some scope. Slight quality has a chance of an infinite
description of quality so it is not really slight quality. The
chance is negligibly against compared to infinity. Quality
is heightened further by appreciation and Christian love.
In the description of the worthwhile are all
worthwhileness's adding up to each worthwhile thing.
The different things are accompanied by different
appropriatenesses in the descriptions. Quality in

knowledge has advantages to knowledge whereas bad in knowledge has disadvantages to knowledge. Life is closer to what it is all about than knowledge, or nature. The advantages of quality and its synonyms are the advantages of nature, when they are of bad they are not enough. If pleasure progresses better than bad it will gain more considerations in its favour than bad for good. Better is good so progress belongs to good. Bad causing good is only partly good.

The attraction of pleasure is a value that possibly multiplies by infinite description. Its description has many benefits and adds value to things. Organised pleasure can progress and be higher than one pleasure, and be more valuable. We need an enchanting life, a positive revolution, a place in God's glory. Joy in journeying through life heightened by celebration. We need more than words can say. The brain needs better making. Good and its synonyms are more appropriate to wants in nature than bad because they have point and positiveness. The description of any of this good, etc. may be infinite. The best moral and right is perhaps further in unknown concepts than in synonyms of right. Right pleasure fits the person and should be all the time or almost if this is practical.

What is the psychology of the wonderful and apply it? Life is composed of finites that each have a chance of an infinite description. Differentiating infinites that exist independently, so adding to more than infinity. Infinite good and pleasure tend to instrumental value and by selection and creation it could have a reasonable amount of good instrumental frequency. Intrinsic good and intrinsic quality are sometimes slight pleasures, sometimes more. Have better brain fit, for better brain use. Quality benefits from the richness that is in all emotion and the plainness that is blended in all emotion can add quality. Quality increases by other quality. Heighten height.

Good during infinite time has larger finites during infinity than bad giving an infinite of more good than bad. Possibly good will be superseded by new concepts but if these cannot do enough, good will still be needed. The more good the finites, the better the infinity.

Niceness has a chance of being in paradise one or more of an infinite number of things better in unfound concepts than the best ultimate. The chance is negligible compared to the infinity the chance has. This is infinitely better than the best ultimate. Infinity is composed of all the finites. If each thing has an infinite description at any finite degree or rareness there would be an infinite number of concepts further than the ultimate placeable in order of merit.

Niceness is the way to get people to paradise not good and bad. Paradise can increase its own numbers better than by leaving to get new people. The chance of infinity or further than infinity is negligible compared to the infinity or further the chance has because the more the chances of, the less significant the chance and this is

4

infinite, or further than infinite, and makes the chance as if certainty.

Utopia is an alternative to paradise. Niceness has meaning and is something compared with nothing and this is shared with all possible steps of meaning. If the steps extend to infinity a share at a finite fraction is still infinite. Infinity itself may be a step in an infinite number of steps. Bad is negligible compared to the good. By tending constantly towards just niceness nastiness will be reduced to a minute fraction of infinity and niceness. Alternatives yet to be found can still be infinite as well.

The subject and infinite number of steps better than scope is improved upon by an infinite number of steps past the infinite. The subject makes the thing partly there.

Positiveness is naturally advantageous to our nature and naturalness is right. Naturalness fits the person. It is a kind of normalness. Negativeness does not usually cause enough good. Right is positive, and generally natural to our nature. Fitting the person is more satisfying. Each thing has the full description of nature because one can always say in describing something "and other things in nature also exist". The differences of things accompanies appropriateness of description. The appropriateness of human nature is that which fits it. Take naturalness happily.

Bad is not an equivalent of good it is its opposite. Good does not need to be explained and verified. As a feeling it is itself. Its synonyms support it. Defining it is needed in communicating the thought – feeling, and for further knowledge feeling is a blend of richness and plainness, but mostly it is itself. As such it can be observed, though if it is semi-aware it may be missed. Good meaning moral is not the only use of the word good. Niceness is intrinsically good and instrumental good, potential and actualised good ,strong, medium and weak and other ways of dividing it up. Value because it can be observed in pleasure, but complexity and lack of repeating observation leads to opinion. Opinion can be based on chance and reason together, so opinion tends to be valuable and tends to progress with more knowledge. Paradise is proper if it adds value according to opinion. The richness that is in emotion gives us all our valuable meaning. Paradise uses love appreciation and blending of niceness with nastiness to make nastiness and heightening become niceness. The blending is simultaneous with the occurrence of the bad. This maybe how God knows nastiness, and knows everything happening. The aliens are not sure we should not have nastiness so we have nastiness before a final decision. This is for the whole world together. This is alien policy about us, and we have been left on our own because it is our nature it is about, and perhaps because nastiness is unpopular with the aliens. Having nastiness may be right for us. If we choose to have niceness and nastiness we will lose scope without the aliens if this is true. In alien

6

natures the atomic may not be the only giant. Aliens are not bodies but mediums, where sensory vision and sensory sound are two of our mediums. Emotion is in different mediums and the atomic we know is possibly a single giant medium.

Paradise can be a free choice.

Morals are right and worthwhile because judgement is better than nothing by observation of its intrinsicness as a word and chance so opinion at least tends to have value. More significant meaning is rich and deep. This emphasises ones choice. Richness is more appropriate to positiveness than negativeness, and depth emphasises this. Advantages are positive not negative almost by definition. Praise magnifies. The aesthetics of paradise are not just beauty but beauty and its synonyms. Each emotion is rich. This gives rise to all known significant meaning and beauty has significant meaning, by observation. Morals are the morals of pleasure which makes morals beautiful, and synonyms.

Pleasure in the beauty of holiness adds value to the subject 'infinitely better than the ultimate of progress or perfection'. Christ in his kind of infinity is the main point instead of needing to be right in good and bad. If there is an infinite description of nature any finite rareness of kind of subject gives an infinite number of subjects better than perfection. Quality and its synonyms as pleasure is developed in general to serve the subject. Good is still progressing or doing better than progress, in a progress

7

direction. Better or further is best done by the subject 'an infinite number of steps further than searching in the best scope'. This is done in pleasure and Christ for further value. A subject makes its things partly there. Christ and God need not be real but mental phenomena which gives them reality but the finite chance of an infinite God equals its certainty and if it doesn't is still valuable. The chance is negligible compared to infinity, becoming less and less significant endlessly. Any pleasure is infinitely valuable, because pleasure has a chance of infinitely better description than nastiness. Just nastiness doesn't progress. The chance is negligible compared to infinity which then equals certainty. The description may go to every finite that composes infinity, infinity is always finite so it does not always cancel out at good and evil each at infinity or possibly whatever good and evil becomes in other concepts. The different feelings have differentiating infinites which add instead of infinite plus infinite equals infinite. A finite fraction differentiating gives an infinite. Subjects are best done by pleasure. They have a chance of an infinite description where the chance is negligible compared to the infinity and also a chance and subject of an infinite number of steps further than value which infinitely further concept is a better infinite and this is included in the chance of its infinitely further description, because its infinity includes that infinity. Any finite rareness in an infinite description gives an infinity of cases of better, if put in an infinite order of precedence, the number of steps extending infinitely further. During an infinite description the description of good will tend to always be bigger and growing more than that for bad. Because good progresses and bad doesn't.

One can say 'pleasure is infinitely better than bad' and the infinity is so important here that it justifies pleasure even if it is a bias. Just saying it is enough.

All subjects can be applied. Good quality and their synonyms can be done in pleasure. Morals are high but there is one main moral, constant satisfying pleasure. Knowledge is good and bad. Naturalness is better. We may be natural compared with the future. Intellect, light and morals can be had within pleasure. Priorities can be found in pleasure. Things in paradise are closer to perfection. The same things enjoyed or enjoyed more. Better classics. The stars are close tonight. One is constantly blessed in paradise.

Love is infinite because it has an infinite description and loves an infinite good nature. If God develops during time love may only become infinitely strong in an infinite time. But there is the subject infinite love and an infinite number of further steps but this may not be love. Description is what a thing is so the description of love is the same as love and the description has a chance of being infinite where the chance is neglectably against compared to infinity and so equals its certainty, with negligible difference. Love needs no cross. The cross is an exception not something to dwell on. Religion brings pleasure but not necessarily constant pleasure.

9

The aliens are the nearest thing to God. The future should not be mistaken for alien. The future has time travelling UFOs and has gone beyond the human being. Christ is an ideal for humanity. The concept God has infinite point. The chance of God equals its certainty since the chance is negligible compared to infinity, but the infinity demands believe. I don't believe in punishing in the afterlife. Paradise does not believe in bads. Paradise is a duty or an acceptable opportunity not a reward. How good is liking compared to Christian love? Loving good is loving God if he exists. There are bigger goods than loving ones neighbour as one's self, which Christ said was the second most important commandment. The bigger goods are found in and from God if he exists. Describing the word God enough perhaps gives it more reality than a certain object without any description given. Aesthetics should be aesthetics of paradise. Some categories give pleasure but the same categories also not. The aesthetic appreciation of nature can be taken as if man created nature and that he didn't. Reality is not simply aesthetically appreciable to our nature as it is good and bad. One has to have a selected reality, but reality can have a limited description limited to pleasure and still refer to the whole of reality. Even perhaps add up to the concept reality since a full description isn't needed to add up to the thing described, except that a more real concept includes bad, except perhaps to God if there is one.

The highest paradise goes to those with the highest income, as incentive to the better ability to serve better.

The bible is not a paradise book because it is good and bad even if the bad is for leaving and not doing. To be in paradise even the subliminal should be pleasure and ideally ones dreaming. Paradise is got by using the brain.

Aim at happiness and pleasure to serve the great subjects, (which are also applied). One such is 'an infinite number of steps past pleasure' which an infinite description might give, at a finite rareness of part. It might be in good or past it in a good direction. Another great subject is 'an infinite number of steps further than infinite pleasure', with an infinite number of steps past infinite. These are keys to God in eternity. The chance of infinity gets less and less significant into infinity compared with infinity and good does it better than bad and good. An infinite further steps for example past quality give better infinites at endless finites in infinity. Compared to just infinite quality or whatever. If quality differentiates endlessly in time this does not equal just infinity. Everything of quality has infinite quality. If nature expands infinitely and keeps differentiating qualities this is infinite times infinite without it equalling just infinity. A finite fraction of infinitely further is infinitely further, so it could cut down to any finite proportion. Better than more scope is better scope, which doesn't need more. Good rather than good and bad will more likely benefit by better scope. Applying the subject produces the real thing, and the real thing helps feed the subject. Quality and synonyms can give more scope than good and bad by better progress. Any quality has the description of all quality including all instrumental quality so intrinsic quality has all instrumental quality in that way. We need medicines for quality and its synonyms not normalness. The brain study of pleasure in conjunction with satisfaction, happiness and quality and its synonyms should be much emphasised. Is normalness really the best way to quality and its synonyms or the study of quality and its synonyms itself? The study of the worthwhile may find a place for normalness in quality.

The atomic is plain. You cannot cause it suffering or pleasure, but known by us it becomes an emotional and sensory matter and only partly the same. What we have is personal reality not atomic reality. The atomic shouldn't dominate your mind. You belong to yourself. There are alternative ways of feeling the atomic, depending on brain and mind. I know the atomic is not part of my experience. I know myself.

Intrinsically only myself. Indirectly the atomic beyond my brain. Those who can make their minds enough do not need to be dominated by none paradise feelings of atomic, but can attempt paradise.

This is the kingdom of power and glory and further. Increasing fulfilment forever and further than fulfilment, in subject. If there is a God with an infinitely meaningful description man has an infinitely meaningful description as he includes the description of God in his description, but it applies more to God. Good has more advantages. Advantages are good. Advantages can give pleasure.

Proper pleasure is more than good. It is an attractive treasure. It fits the person. It does not go against the nerves. It has positive richness and meaning. It tends to beauty. It is more lovable than just good, more wantable. Its strength heightens these things. Positiveness is something with meaning. Bad is worse than no meaning and further from positiveness than nothing or neutral - which is halfway between positiveness and bad. Pleasure is positive, nastiness negative. Nastiness can be said to have meaning which is negative.

Light is creative. Creativity has life. Life has knowledge.

Morals are readily done in paradise. They have to be nice and completely wanted. Satisfaction is constant. It is enough to be satisfied. The self is loved as much as ones neighbour. Christ said 'love your neighbour as yourself'. This does not require serving them always equally. There are more important things than for one neighbour, for groups of people. These are done with God, or without belief.

Religion is raising. Also, the bible says "where your heart is there is ones treasure". If an ideal paradise is impossible there is the next best thing. Research should be able to do it. Wanting Christ makes one want heaven. Wanting pleasure can lead to wanting moral sinless pleasure. The bible says though not together "Grace and peace to you from God our Father and the Lord Jesus Christ. Be filled with the fruit of righteousness that comes through Jesus Christ to the glory and praise of God.

Rejoice in the Lord always. Whatever is true. Whatever is noble. Whatever is right. Whatever is pure. Whatever is lovely. Whatever is admirable if anything is excellent or praiseworthy, think about such things," and I say take them infinitely further. Have pleasures which satisfy the soul.

I do not believe sin is punished without faith. This is because paradise is the answer, so much further may your ideals become exalted and practiced, or be in majesty, or touched with glory. If civilisation is to go further upwards, paradise should be attempted.

All atomic quality is instrumental to experience. Feeling can vary for the some atomic experience.

Opinion tends to be valuable since any judgement is better than none and the study of judgement will provide a better basis.

A joy from God is endowed with infinity. The full consciousness of suffering is in God and is possibly joy, so suffering may not exist. The divine should enchant. Quality of life is what matters about quality. Each definition of quality could be a separate science. Treasure, meaning and point can be put together. Holiness and quality can be put together. Religious grace and other grace can be put together. If you can be better in your good, heart and reason are both helpful. Love is helped by liking.

Pleasure incentivises itself. Positiveness has a better brain use and happiness tends to give health.

Natural randomness, biological factors and artisticness limited by technology are mixed in natural good design. The artificial is not always opposed to the natural. How do we do better at living as civilised animals? Is civilisation making us less and less natural? Automate work you don't like. Try work enhancements instead of less work, or with a nicer work increase in work time. Tool design could be given game aspects. Choice can help naturalness. The millions of past years have helped us. Buildings that adapt to summer and winter more an advantage. The natural is tolerant of itself and is free and easy.

More pleasure than otherwise is not a larger total, which is infinite, but larger during infinity, which is better. Soon paradise by proper drugs will become practical and a paradise that does not lessen atomic ability, even increases it. However, progress will only produce paradise if bad for good and good are replaced by pleasure, and this may not happen unless it is done on purpose.

The bible is not very high. Just good appears better and better. Beauty improves religion. Beauty can have meaning more than simply beauty so that the truth is supported. The positive particular emphasises. There is a kinship of beauty and religion. Selected beauty is moral. Beauty is a pleasure and can be a wonder. There is no beauty without feeling. Plato believed beauties participate in the ideal beauty. It shouldn't be 'truth, goodness and beauty' but goodness and good truth and good beauty, and synonyms. Christian grace is a beauty.

If God is in each thing, each thing is infinite.

Beauty has its own truth and goodness. Its truth, though, is not always expressible. The arts raise compared with reality but they don't always go far enough.

The real self has the natural fitting things, which are more good.

There is one right to lots of wrongs but knowledge contains them all. Intrinsic good is obvious certain good but instrumental good has opinion as a disadvantage. Good and good that is only would be bad does approximate reality. A better appropriate description of advantages in good compared to bad and good in a finite proportion extended to infinity is infinitely better; and there is a chance of this infinity that is negligible compared to infinity so that it is as if certain. Infinity is finite throughout so it always beats the infinite less appropriate description of advantages of bad and good. By the finites during infinity being better. Bad doesn't produce enough good. The less bad the less significant its infinity, in chance of description.

Selected pleasures for the self are best for effect on other people.

Paradise is the most wantable condition available and can be made the best simply by saying "paradise is infinitely better than good or bad and good. " Saying this has a lot of value due to the word infinitely.

How about a mixture of brain boosting and pleasure and more happiness by proper drugs?

If good has disadvantages it is good and bad, and if bad has advantages it is bad and good.

About quality is also about paradise.

Love is better than liking.

Intrinsic good and intrinsic quality are pleasures though they can be very slight pleasures. Choose a subject or treatment of subject for height not reality, except the reality of height. In spiritual faith we may hope well of the truth. Good is a power with many attributes. Proper pleasure is the main form of good. It has proper appeal as well as good; intrinsic good as well as any other good.

Pleasure and advantages are both positive so are related but nastiness and advantages are negative and positive so are not related or not related much.

The subject 'infinitely better than infinite glory' is a very valuable subject in paradise. An infinite number of steps further than the concept infinite glory is obtained if concepts and inferences in it occur at any finite rareness in an infinite description, or subject.

17

All dreams and visions of paradise are places in paradise because they are of pleasure.

Leaving wrong leads to natural right.

The description of everything is in each thing because one can say in describing, 'everything else is' and give everything else, and this puts all the good in bad, but it is barely appropriate. Likewise all of the bad is in good, but it is barely appropriate.

Pleasure is our most intrinsically positive experience. Helpful to happiness. The stronger incentive to the lesser when worthwhile. Happiness has a number of known advantages. Right pleasure is moral and useful.

Positive meaning and its synonyms, and the chance of an infinite number of further steps beyond it, is best, including an infinite number of steps past infinite past steps past past, past chance and past further. This is a subject. There is a chance of a suitable infinite description and finite rareness of concept in the whole of its infinity giving infinite concepts. The subject is done in pleasure for further value.

In a manmade paradise religion is only for those who want it.

Good is more alive than bad.

Continuous quality improvement should aim at paradise. Intrinsic quality is the most real quality, not instrumental quality which causes intrinsic quality. Intrinsic quality causing intrinsic quality is a short cut and so more economical, and meaning is arrived at. Intrinsic quality is a pleasure and pleasure is a synonym of quality. There is appreciation of appreciation; which heightens and other improvements.

If there is an infinite description of pleasure then there are probably an infinite number of considerations in its evaluation and infinite value of pleasure except that infinity is always finite throughout. Description refers to nature. Description of wrong and end is not wantable. My description is in relevancies to aspects of nature.

The aim of just knowledge does not progress instead of progress. One just collects or goes through knowledge.

Right is natural right. The quality direction shows more promise than bad and so more likely more alternatives than bad.

Pleasure may last forever, if time is never finished, but the subject can include the whole of infinite time.

Nothing is just good in description but there are kinds of good including intrinsic good and pleasure. Religion is in favour of paradise. Reason is in favour of paradise. Paradise is also desirable. The intellect is heightened. It is loveable. It is infinite. It goes to the wonderful. It enhances its beginning and sources. It is utopian and has many characteristics of other utopias. It is a great

19

treasure. It has dimensional scent, and other highness. It is a constant blessing. Danger is considerably less.

The subject infinitely further than quality in a quality direction is served by quality. Intrinsic quality is a pleasure.

Intrinsic good is just good but its description adds up to it and contains bad because it contains the description of the whole of nature because one can say 'they rest of things are so and so'; when describing it. Perfection and the ultimate of progress also contain their opposites. Fortunately the bad and opposites have little relevance. Avoid bad description when you can.

Beauty can warm the heart. Nobleness has a practical beauty. Pleasure has a light.

The best aim is not in knowledge but is an infinite number of steps beyond knowledge which has a chance negligible compared to infinity at any finite rareness of concept in an infinite description. Also aim can be infinitely superseded, in the same way. The subject is done in pleasure for further value.

If God's world is to happen we must give up bad for good. Bad to lessen bad can put bad back into description from which it came, unless it is intrinsic in the first place.

An infinite number of steps beyond infinite quality gives a better infinity in the finites composing infinity. One infinity includes an infinity of differentiating infinites. Add to this the subject of infinity further than differentiating infinities, on the positive side (or positive superseded). Advantages and good are both positive and bad is negative. This alone is enough reason for good. Good makes a better gamble at the unknown than bad.

Any improvement in quality or a synonym of quality is an improvement in infinity. The description that is meaningful infinitely improves. Infinite value is not the limit. During infinity can vary in value.

The description of quality and its synonyms can be said to include further and other than quality because everything is in its description as one can say in describing it every other thing is described. Quality or a synonym of quality comes into every subject but bad is not wantable. Even neutralness has a quality description, and can have instrumental quality.

The chance of infinity is negligible compared to infinity because the chance gets less and less significant into infinity, becoming infinitely small in significance. There is a chance of infinitely further than meaning. Most concepts are unknown. There is no end to searching or progress. Searching can never find its goal since the set of things is endless. Endless progress has a chance of being an answer, and causing infinitely further than progress.

I suggest the descriptive sequence could begin quality then excellent quality then holiness with an appropriate description holiness with a high description supreme holiness and then the chance of infinitely further. The chance of God is worth a religion. Paradise has positive meanings that add to the intellect but are not thought. The richness found in all emotion (feeling) gives rise to 'meaning'. Bad has the opposite of worthwhile meanings. Many feelings can only be named or described in madness. Most feelings in sanity cannot be named or described and sometimes can pass by unnoticed by thoughts and the thoughts orientated self. The brain can divide the feelings of individual words up and produce new combinations that are unreal words. At any rate feelings are a largely unknown territory with each case of feeling having s different life of its own. Paradise would be within this. We don't know the fullness of the beyond. If we go to paradise the animals for one thing, would be made different in the new world. Meditation can help produce happiness. William Blake said 'if the doors of perception were cleansed all things would appear infinite.'

Pleasure with a little exceptional bad could be a science.

Morals can be consistent with paradise.

Certainty is limited but chance is free to go beyond infinity where perfection is not the limit, but unknown concepts, or existences.

Knowledge or good is a gamble. Good may give the most knowledge by progressing better.

Good has little appropriateness too bad as it is the opposite. Almost bad is very little good. May the world become happy, blessed and glorious. People should become wonderful. Going to paradise should be an aim of scientific endeavour.

Emotion and so pleasure is a vibration higher than sound. It has formula. It has content and presence. It all has richness. It has consciousness. It has degrees of strength. It has variety and parts of this variety come and go.

We should be ourselves not go in for just knowledge. The real self has the most appropriate things. Appropriateness can increase good.

Everything is nasty, nice or neutral. Bad has negative meaning which isn't any use. The amount of good caused by bad improves the less bad there is. If bad has advantages leave bad for advantages.

Pleasure, wellbeing, a more positive health, flourishing, good and good point, and positive meanings, done together. The best of this is a paradise.

There is a chance one can go beyond infinity for one reason at least. That infinity is always finite being composed of an infinite number of finites. Infinite subjects are done in pleasure for further value. The subjects include the endless but finding steps one is always with an infinity ahead if in infinite time. The subject is better than finding steps.

Pleasure can stand out. Paradise is more positive than just good. Pleasure has what all things have including being and cause and effect. It has life. The atomic has an alternative to life. Mind has places with it. Emotion is more alive than the sensory experience. Humanity may not need to aim at just the best or ultimate. It could make a contribution to a possible wider way.

Progress might pass by the ultimate available to progress without actually entering it, for better of further as yet unfound concepts. The ultimate would be a good place to do infinite subjects. Pleasure gives the best chance of an ultimate as it is the best quality and good while quality and good progress better without bad except exceptions. Searching for the ultimate of progress in just knowledge only gives a chance of this ultimate. The ultimate of progress because the ultimate is otherwise acceptable or unacceptable. Progress either increases good and lessens bad or increases bad and increases the good more than the bad. To go to paradise there is a need to lessen nastiness and not want by causing pleasure and want satisfaction instead.

There is a chance of an infinitely valuable description adding up to the thing described, which can be pleasure.

There is the subject and chance of pleasure going an infinite number of concept steps beyond infinity and still being pleasure, but infinity can include that. Beyond concepts are actual full or fuller forms of reality, things concepts can refer to. There is a chance God has all of them and we play a useful part, and have a chance of an infinite number of them, whether all or not, by progress. At any finite rareness there is an infinite number of realities better than infinite value of pleasure, getting better endlessly, in an infinite suitable description in a chance negligible compared to infinity as if infinity was certain. One can add to infinite value possibly beyond value by a far enough subject and chance. Pleasures add the finites of more than one differentiating infinity. The infinite description of pleasure can be any finite slightness of value per part and add up to infinite value.

The subjects infinite progress and infinite scope are better than finite progress and finite scope but ordinary progress and scope can add value to subjects and their uses, and these subjects should be done within them. The same applies to infinite steps beyond progress and scope.

Eternity is greater than we can conceive. Gods glory passes all understanding but we have an important part to play, however slight in comparison.

Entertainment isn't just pleasure, and its pleasure is generally not much. Want satisfaction can be more. Quality in pleasure makes life worth living. Paradise can have more meaning. Paradise becomes wonderful. Entertainment in paradise is a different matter. Be pure in heart. Most fiction belongs to good and bad. Drugs may be capable of giving a more positive health not just pleasure, a more positive health than health.

People in paradise work for passion rather than money. The morals require pleasure. Wellness of mind assists moral goodness. Pleasure causes pleasure. It is not opinion of what is pleasant but observation. Some people find one things pleasant and satisfying some another. Bad is worse than useless. Wellness of mind is greatest in paradise. Pleasure always has beauty in it. Quality in pleasure has more meaning.

Progress in good is better than difficulty and effort. Better good survived better than difficulty in evolution and survived better than bad because of its advantages. Difficulty and effort, if part of good, as causes of better, was a small part of good, and couldn't become emphasised.

The mind is too complicated for quick progress if this becomes possible. It would go wrong too much. People wouldn't know well enough what they are doing. There are the feelings of the atomic and other feelings and their partial permutations. This is vast. A lot to deal with.

The advantages of paradise are infinite. Progress may be for an infinite time, or superseded time. God may be more fully infinite. The atomic and mind may not be the only two things, and paradise may be the main condition. Intrinsic positiveness is treasure and negativeness the opposite of treasure. Better positiveness is better treasure. Pleasure given to millions or thousands of people can be a very small improvement per person but significant in total. Sometimes the main scientific theory should lead authority, sometimes freedom to follow different opinions is correct. This is also true in paradise. Morals are justified by the weight of, or the language of, quality and its synonyms. Quality and its synonyms are justified by their advantages. The point of advantages is self-evident.

The subject further than the positive ultimate is helped by advantages. The chance of a positive ultimate at infinity is negligible compared to infinity so it is as if certain. Paradise is an ultimate that can give advantages further than the positive ultimate. The subject includes all its finite steps into infinity whereas further steps are only finite, finite continuing perhaps endlessly. Past the ultimate is in unfound concepts at any finite rareness in an infinite description, finites extending endlessly.

Anything is an ultimate because of the chance of an infinite ultimate in description the chance being negligibly against.

'Beauty is truth, truth beauty. That is all we know on earth and all we need to know.'

Evil is avoided by enough thought or a good heart. Wrong is left for natural right, our natural selves are our right selves. Paradise is the most fulfilling place. Christians are asked to copy heaven. There is little scope in low good. An instrumental good is either intrinsically good or intrinsically bad or neutral. If good progresses better than bad the proportion of bad should tend to lessen. We need advantages. The point of advantages is self-evident.

You can do a whole infinity and still have infinity left out.

Although nice all the time less nice can cause more nice. Glory in nature has meaning. Holiness brings joy. 'The joy of the lord is your strength.' Gain a deep commitment and passion for living.

Ease achieves more than effort and is nicer. Beauty is appreciateable. Appreciation heightens. Christian love heightens. Belief in God heightens. Things that can be appreciated heighten and better is appreciated more. Knowledge is to make us. If similar to God it should make us good, and in constant pleasure, and the sooner the better. Would be bads instead of bads allow pleasure of all things. Pleasure is part of good. Good is part of quality. Quality is part of good. Intrinsic quality without nastiness is always a pleasure.

Quality has infinitely more considerations in favour than bad for good in an infinite description. Strictly speaking this is always finite as infinity is an endless sequence of finites. So it doesn't just have an infinite set of considerations for and against which cancel out.

If one is not to do bad for good one cannot sacrifice for the sake of others. A beautiful soul does not ignore the world's morals if such a mind is moral. Moral complexity of good and bad disappears, becoming wrongs, which are not beautiful and not to be known. A beautiful mind is enough, though I add synonyms. Right goes to quality, and quality is right, and more than right, in unfound concepts. The possibility of these is to make a difference. If there is an infinite description there is possibly an infinite number of considerations, together giving infinite value and any acceptable alternatives to right.

Quality and good are a better part of normal. Niceness and want satisfaction is partly from nice upbringing, is partly from ones genes, partly by what books one reads, partly by the making mind, partly by intelligence and memory, partly by good circumstances and environment, all of which can be improved and chances can be increased. Other people can help. Competition and cooperation can be channelled. Truth lasts. We are more than great. Attempt wisdom, justification and properness. Beauty illuminates the mind, raises the imagination and warms the heart. Providing the best meaning each moment is the chief concern, the best one can do. Beauty does not need to be a utility. It still benefits in meaning. Meaning is served by and is the point of the instrumental. Reason supports quality and good and their synonyms. Quality is the sign of the quality direction, that may have an infinite number of steps beyond quality; in an infinite description at any finite rareness of concept. A finite number could take a thousand miles to write down, by the briefest method.

Possibly in the unconscious all our nastiness are blended with enough niceness, and this is the reality not nastiness. Meaning goes further from chaos than order, order without meaning is pointless and niceness has the most positive meaning. If symmetry and order and proportion are in beauty it is because they are raised by the mind. Beauty can take the form of knowledge and knowledge can be limited by desire for good which can make knowledge beautiful. Experience is not chaotic, neither is beauty or niceness. Beauty has resplendence of form. There are different ways of dividing things up. This applies to ways of attempting to create paradise.

Knowledge doesn't always fit the subject but one cannot say what will fit the completed subject. So any knowledge of the subjects is worth adding.

Positive meaning is better than negative meaning which is worse than no meaning. Better or worse may be superseded and not in their direction. An alternative to bad need not be bad or good.

Beauty is not just quantity, and takes many angles, forms. Transcendental accomplishments are high, and improved with passion. Beauty is not an understanding but an understood thing can be beautiful. One can imagine beauty.

One's point should be one's life.

For pleasure go up, climatise. Tune the mind in, prepare, 'leave wrongs, harmonise, be appropriate, make, find niceness, be neutral, take proper drugs, find gold in the mind, help each other open the heaven gate, be versatile, smile, do work you like, be happy, perhaps have Christian love, improve, make worth, maintain your joy, disassociate yourself from bad, be positive, shine, have wellbeing, sing, be easy and satisfy.

Try to make a practical paradoxical utopia. Believe in beauty. Find inspiration. Start and continue support. Be holistic.

Go further by progress not by difficulty. Take your time. Social welfare is your welfare.

If infinite time exists although endless is all there. Take care about the future. Reality to us now is good and bad but good is the point.

Height and dedication gives great lovely and immortal works.

The religious person should have liberty and happiness with God. If you go in for just knowledge it is to see what it will find. Infinitely better than knowledge is a subject. Its chance of truth is negligibly against compared to infinity.

Right is the best of good, possibly further. Do pleasure and want satisfaction. If there are steps further than paradise they are all something compared to nothing and negativeness. Paradise is something. Quality is something. Negativeness is further than nothing in a nothing direction. If we find an ultimate or other ending it will not be absolutely infinitely certain and the chance of an infinite number of further steps will be nothing

31

compared to its infinity so it will be as certain. Infinity is always finite with an infinity ahead. Paradise adds further point, value, meaning and good to subjects, and their use.

Everything is not beautiful. The atomic is plain though it can make us feel positive or negative. There is no sadness in pleasure ending if it is replaced by other pleasure.

Good goes to pleasure. A large knowledge of good may create a paradise. Good as morals is only one thing that can help. Good heightened, or refined can be in paradise. More good means more happiness, and more of possible God. Grace becomes a full life of pleasure. We enjoy pleasure because it has intrinsic value. This has meaning. How fortunate that the universe contains positive meaning, that can be emphasised. It has positive significance and treasure. Existence and so meaning must be more reasonable than nothing and both are inevitable in their reasonably caused being. Nature is full of reasons. Nature behaves reasonably. Red and white make pink. This is reasonable. Likewise in the rest of nature. Meaning is reasonable. It is also alive. There is no escaping the laws and forces of nature but we can put them to use determined by reason and quality and its synonyms, I hope, in paradise giving them more meaning. Meaning is more positive than negative and positive meaning can be distinguished.

Positive meaning exists because existence exists. Variety would come across meaning. In the human case from the richness that is in all emotion. Description is the same as the thing described so beauty is a possible infinite description.

Reality includes the immoral, so don't have reality. It is opinion whether bad is worth having or how much to have. Good is a chance worth taking and may go an infinite number of steps past the best in unfound concepts, perhaps past good and bad and their synonyms. It is moral to have paradise. It is not a reward. It is a creation of man and God. Be more natural. Reality is not naturalness. Knowledge is reality.

There is no wrong bias against bad by good. It acts as an incentive due to advantages being positive not negative. Suffering has its own discouragement. Positive meaning has significance and meaning beyond that conveyed by language. Infinite positive meaning can be more than bad during infinity of time since infinity is always finite being composed of an infinite number of finites. The description is more during its infinity since it contains the description of the better progress of positiveness than bad, also potential progress. Positive meaning is more in paradise. Paradise enhances the richness found in all of feeling and it is richness which gives rise to meaning. Plain blended with richness gives more scope.

The definition of anything including quality and pleasure is the description of it. This is all classification and attributes and parts of a construction. It takes less than the full description to add up to the thing described.

The rest of nature is in the description of anything so all of nature is in the description and although it is all appropriate it gets very slightly so indirectly.

At a pound per person there would be several billions of pounds to try and make paradise practical.

There is the subject 'progress according to a further than infinitely meaningful description of progress.' Also infinitely further than progress in a progress direction.

Beauty should be limited by truth. Love is not the only positive meaning, unless you mean positive meaning. To love is to like, but better than to like. Love is a beauty. Love your neighbour as much as yourself, not more than yourself. The best possible has superior merit; and should have soundness. Though sometimes it is little better than the next best but this is almost as desirable, and sometimes should be done next.

Brain enhancement can be done without drugs, by several methods. Create nearer paradise, if you can't create paradise. Love should support joy and good. God and man teach and make. If civilisation behaves positively nature is positive. Use methods of avoiding bads. Sometimes this just means lessening bad. Reduce bad to exceptions. Find good things to extrapolate. Variety is the spice of life, good is better than salt. Be rich in good and its synonyms. Appreciation and love and inspiration can be more than words can give. Good includes little danger. Sometimes invest in the long term. Good can fail sometimes, bad is a failure. End or leave bad, but don't usually seek it out for that purpose. Causing good will prevent bad being caused.

If one dies consciousness in other people may continue enough, instead.

Properly empower the source of good things, make them efficient at good, leaving things to God should not prevent us from being the servants of God. The available can be found. Joy to you, joy from you, joy at you. Problems can be good or bad. Perseverance should be in good only. Grace and morals are high and this serves. A pure heart raises. Happiness helps allow grace because happiness and grace are both positive. Do dancing more than marching, through life. Good is a strength. Aim at constant positive wholeness. Joy can be satisfied without Christ and still be proper although opinion. Hardship and struggle are said to produce maturity but we are told that we need to be like children to enter heaven.

Causes of paradise need to avoid disadvantages. Add normal positiveness to holiness. The want of good gives rise to the want of more good.

Paradise has good in pleasure, pleasure in good, and pleasure in pleasure.

The proportion of bad can lessen while the same bad increases.

Advantages are positive not negative and are best for finding other than advantages in unfound concepts.

Bigger steps into infinity make the finites that compose infinity larger and so a bigger infinity. Steps of bigger quality are an advantage.

For every right there are a number of wrong alternatives so that knowledge is mostly about wrong. Doing intrinsic quality and its synonyms puts a limit on this, one can assume intrinsic quality and its synonyms are a right limit.

The point of good is not unselfishness but good itself.

Likeableness should be given unreal perfection. Real perfection would be more than infinite and unlikely. Unreal perfection is more than excellence. Real perfection with an infinite number of further steps can be a chance. The subject makes it partly there by aspects of its nature, but unreal perfection is needed for added value. Real perfection is more than infinitely better. But getting better endlessly will never reach perfection though this may be perfection and this is better than infinite perfection as may go beyond infinity. Infinity completes itself but is It always finite. Good being better than bad is better at the unknown. There is an infinite number of infinite descriptions of quality and pleasure in infinity in the chances of meaningful description. Taking the quality and pleasure direction further and further. The description adds up to the thing described because the description is the same as the thing described. Such positive things are in the appropriate description of pleasure. Subjects further than pleasure can be done in paradise for further value.

Good progressing better than bad is in favour of just good intentionally. God is good, not good and bad, and cannot properly cause bad for good. Bad for good is in the opinion that enough good is sometimes caused by intentional bad.

Perhaps morals are not absolute because immortality can be forgiven. Better or alternative to better than infinity is done in infinity so is part of a more than infinite value of infinity. The endless is complete to be infinite.

The appropriate description of pleasure is just pleasure without bad. The less and non-appropriate description is the rest of being except perhaps in the unknown.

The point of religion is to have good for thousands or millions of people from God or oneself with God not unselfishness towards individuals which is of minor importance. Moral beauty is only partly unselfishness. There is a sharing in the divine holy image. Incentive to serve the millions is acceptable. Moral being can be heightened. Moral beauty benefits from beauty. It helps happiness which has benefits of happiness. The proper self is divine. Morals are capable of being beautiful. Beauty enhances morals. Forgiveness gives freedom. Holiness does not violate that freedom but each person wears a crown. Morals may not be absolute because of forgiveness but forgiveness is moral. Absoluteness is a kin to the ultimate; but only one step in infinity. There are unfound concepts and other unfound changes.

Slow can bring more with it and give more scope. It also tends to affect and benefit a longer time, and can take more steps to be right. Less valuable things are added as well as more valuable for a larger total value. Able slow development is quicker progress.

More value than otherwise for a short time if progress is infinitely lasting increases the value all along the line of values during time. Adding to the value of the world means there is more value in nature in a future estimate.

Nothing then point then something wonderful naturally follows in that direction. Then an infinite number of further steps. The subject makes this partly there. The subject contains parts of its nature. Wonderful holiness is a next step. Right is superseded. If there are an infinite number of steps a finite proportion gives an infinite number of steps in paradise. Finiteness extends throughout infinity this applies to other subjects with infinite steps. The word infinity can feel of the nature of infinity. I have felt it this way.

Quality in pleasure is both quantifiable and not quantifiable, depending on the meaning of quality words. Quantities can be subjective approximates.

Moral paradise is better than just goodness. Holy paradise better still but the two could mix for more value.

More scope increases the chances of finding further than holy paradise in a holy paradise direction or further than moral paradise in a moral paradise direction. Right goes to paradise because pleasure adds more positive meaning. Appreciate and celebrate satisfying pleasure.

There is always infinitely more at each finite in infinity. Infinite positive description plus infinite positive description increases each finite value in infinity. Infinity is composed of an infinite number of infinites. Descriptions add their value to total nature. The descriptions are instantaneous on the things described, descriptions being the same thing as the thing described. If a thing is incompletely described just put 'and the rest of its nature' to end describing it, though this has little intrinsic meaning, compared to complete description. Pleasures have a chance of an infinitely meaningful description the chance being negligible compared to infinity and one can add them together in value, instead of infinite value plus infinite value equalling infinite value, because the infinites differentiate or add finites.

The truth contains the answer but is not the answer because it has the truth of right and wrong, and is mostly wrong because for every right there are alternatives. Doing anything leaves out most of nature. Scope could be more by limiting to progress of quality and its synonyms. Quality also gives meaning to an infinite number of steps further than quality, because it is needed to do it and an infinite number of steps beyond progress can progress. The holy and moral are synonyms of quality and improve

39

quality and the other synonyms. The concept infinity takes them to further concepts. The chance of infinity is negligible compared to infinity. The ability to progress in good is a great ability. During progress with its infinite number of further steps beyond progress in a progress direction has the subject better than infinite progress.

Go in for just pleasure and want satisfaction, with progress transcendence will come. Description all boils down to one thing, aspects of God, who has infinite description as intrinsic experience or the equivalent. This is a chance like a certainty, the chance being negligible but alternatively it needs making by progress in nature. The subject infinite development puts infinity partly there by aspects of its nature. A fraction of infinity is an infinity itself and this the subject has. The subject is an infinite economy, and can grow to infinite in an infinite time. There is nothing, then forgiveness, then an infinite number of further steps, and nothing, then morals, then an infinite number of further steps in unfound knowledge. The more value the better so one should be great. Chances of infinity can be worthwhile even if the chances are not negligible compared to infinity.

Opinion of good is alright as long as it is in pleasure. Christ does not have to say all that he is made to say in the bible. Opinion is often the best answer available, in a matter. It can be based on judgement.

Personified good and personified further than good is higher and so is a reason why a God.

Not much need be done to find steps beyond pleasure in a pleasure direction because the subject 'an infinite number of steps than pleasure in its direction' is better, and this is better than an actual finite number of steps.

The idea that pleasure should be in moderation is because we have not learnt to do any better. The idea that denial of pleasure leads to spiritual growth is partly at least for dealing with bad.

Right living leads to further advantages because advantages are positive and largely unstated. Likewise wrong living gives further disadvantages, not the punishment of God. Judgement is worthwhile as a chance. A chance is positive compared with nothing. There is more chance of the ultimate as a positive advantage that a satisfactory negative. A chance of an infinite number of further steps may go further that infinitely further and includes the chance of an infinite number of steps past infinity.

The atomic was allowed or created from potential, possibly. The atomic has no point in itself but can be used by other natures and give rise to 'richness.' Emotion is a 'richness.' The atomic has minimum beings which are not infinitely small but comparable to the minimum beings of vision, like points but bigger than a thousandth of an inch. The microscopic is not smaller than you can see but less large, possibly. Richness is nearer to treasure, and so paradise, than the opposite of treasure. Constant treasure near in paradise suggests there is more scope of

41

emotion in paradise than in bad. Build and develop quality.

Fitting nature is like fitting the truth so we should fit the person as part of nature. The truth is all of knowledge known and unknown. A man made paradise fitting nature is on the good side and could be nearer God, perhaps put as in touch with God. The possibility of God is a great advantage. Have happiness pleasure and want satisfaction. These fit the person best, of what we have.

Nature progresses whether it knows or not, apart from in man, so it does have meaning. Brain combinations of circuits in development have not been slow as evolution appears to be slow. The animals are worth keeping. Unnatural behaviour doesn't fit the brain.

Evil and good are not entirely distinct but are real opposites. Both are described by the fullness of nature but the description appropriate to good is not appropriate to evil.

Richness as in all emotion gives rise to more meaning in paradise I expect, due to more progress and perhaps more size perhaps wanted in progress.

The chance of an infinite has the finite compared to the infinite, giving an infinite difference.

Infinite variety of language may be possible because there are numbers that vary to infinity. The chance is sufficient as it is negligible compared to infinity, so it is as of it was certain. The whole of nature is in the description of anything as one can say in describing "other things are so and so" and name them. This is an infinite description containing all the numbers. Quality includes the description of an infinite number of steps further than progress. Progress may go further than quality in a quality direction. Holiness does better than quality and needs progress and further as its infinity is in time, and God may be developing in time. Alien paradises and neutral natures and negatives without bad are perhaps made and allowed. There is a chance of an infinite number of steps further than holiness in a holy direction. It doesn't matter how small the chance is.

Be particular to have pleasure. Be attracted, high, alive enough and positive. Remember the nature of niceness. Be positively well. Go in for intrinsic quality, and niceness within different niceness, and repeating niceness making different combinations. Be positively right, and good. Go in for advantages and meaning and do these when wanted. Increase happiness. Treasure beauty. Love good, naturalness, ease, relaxation, holiness, halcyon days, goldenness, flower gardens. Imitate high society. Go to the opera. Enchant, attempt excellence, enhance grace. Have a part and so on. Start a paradise library. Don't let things turn you down. Partake of the riches within. Make a kingdom of God. Progress into it, whether God is real or not. Moral perfection is not needed. Morals in paradise are easy, they have to be nice and completely wanted. The kingdom of God should be

43

open to non-believers as well as believers. Good things in paradise for some holy things for others. Sometimes the same thing is both. Paradise serves the great subjects and their use.

Fine arts refine purifying thought, and add to the inner life. Showing finer revelations of God.

Paradise includes the most positive experiences available apart from infinity and no maximum, as well.

There is a chance and subject of infinitely further of each word in an infinite description of pleasure so that finite steps in infinity of description become infinite. Appropriate description alone counts not bad. Cutting infinity by infinity for loss of bad is no real loss as still an infinite quantity remains.

Advantages add to the size of good, compared to bad and increase by progress. Paradise will fulfil you, and more than fulfil you. It will fill you with riches beyond your wildest dreams. Good beyond measure, exaltation, holy holy holy enchantment, dreams to reality, wonder, love, elation, ecstasy, light, moral ease, and everything taken as better than infinite or further than best in new or unfound concepts, and progress to still further. Strength of pleasure is not so much the point as the degree of quality and good of pleasure. An attempt at paradise would be better than outer space for people's money.

Morals have advantages. Increasing ability increases moral ability. Ability is a useful skill. Usefulness is a

44

matter of advantages. Advantages have point, and meaning. The most advantage is the best, in any situation with advantages.

Paradise has greater meaning and ultimates probably have greater meaning.

Scope may find better or an alternative to better but value and its synonyms already has something and we don't know how far it can extend; so value may be a better gamble than scope. An infinite number of further steps including past infinity and past value and its synonyms is an even better gamble; done in paradise. The subject makes it partly there, and the chance is as if certain.

If in infinity good becomes infinitely greater than bad, bad in nature is reduced to an infinitely small proportion a proportion at infinity has an infinite difference.

Because advantages progress better than bad, bad will become exceptions, if paradise is not aimed at.

Meaning will prevent the universe ending in chaos.

If paradise fits our nature better than non-paradise then the future will be a paradise. This requires harmony, or not clashing with our basic nature. Christ believed in good and evil. He says in the bible 'blessed are ye, when men shall revile you and persecute you and shall say all manner of evil against you falsely, for my sake.' Again 'whosever will come after me let him deny himself and take up his cross and follow me.' This is contradicted in 'ye shall find rest unto your souls. For my yoke is easy and my burden is light.' Our bible has a lot about evil in it which makes it half evil.

Would be bads can be without bad. They can be done without realising they are would be bads.

Do better to better still and sometimes a mixture of both. Practical faith is improved by practice based on theory. If Christ is to live in your life one has to learn. If religion is good its aims are good, if one can find the right ones but opinion is enough. Have peace add ease. Aim at glory not temptation. God in us is a treasure. Be pure, it is intrinsically higher. Have faith in importance, and further, maintenance and progress needed in better and further. Be enriched. Intrinsically love is only one word in the description of nature. Love adds meaning. Development towards God will continue in a man-made paradise. Selecting within help should mean more achieved. Pleasant work is liberating, energy adding and capable of a lesser wage. Acceptability has to do with meaning or an alternative to meaning. Infinitely past meaning is needed. Infinity includes an infinite number of infinites in the one infinity.

Have a rich helpful life. Experience a new and greater nature. Use the gifts of grace. Live deeply. Recline in paradise. Have care or love. Go light direct to further light.

Bad for good is not best because advantages are positive not negative.

Trying to find an answer is not the point but an infinite number of steps past answering as a subject and chance. Steps at an angle are counted. Fitting the person's nature has a chance of fitting an infinite amount of knowledge of human nature, in description. Human nature includes all the knowledge we find. Bad is the opposite of good not just poor, and doesn't fit our nature.

Meaning is positive meaning. Negative meaning is further than nothing from something. Quality and its synonyms are something. You need a choice of advantages.

High normalness is paradisiacal. Bad is more imperfect than less good still good. The best good is generally with a number of alternative lesser goods and bads. Love of good gives meaning to good. One does not love bad. Just love means loving good and bad persons.

Positiveness motivates, and should do. If man can create paradise it is wonderful, at least. Not having love is neutral it is not wanting a good, not evil. Good has more size than bad by better progress and these goods are in its description, before progress arrives at them.

The description of things is there going beyond things we know because it is the same as the thing described and the thing described is there. Bad in the description of good need not be known. The bad in the description of good becomes good in a way because the description is the same as the thing described. Paradise has a negligible chance against of an infinite ultimate and infinitely further in its description. Paradise also has intrinsic value to give it meaning with a chance of infinitely further than infinity of intrinsic value. There is a chance and subject of an infinite number of great advantages or further of paradise. The description would be there because it is the same as the thing described, paradise. To be healed is to enter paradise and to be enabled to stay in that state. One cannot say beforehand what in paradise will add to the main subjects so general paradise is required. Maximum holiness, perfection and the ultimate of progress and further are steps mixed in infinity. The finites during infinites add together so the infinites add. Infinites themselves can add by differentiating without infinite plus infinite equalling infinity.

We should have paradise because it is moral. Knowledge and its application can be limited by advantages and further. Love can mean one is largely made. Celebrate the disciplines. Learn wisdom. Enough philosophy and you get religion. The good of the self is the main ingredient that makes life worth living.

If there is a God in charge of affairs, it has become time for infinity to be prominent in the new way. Eternity is added. Nothing is something to the mind or we could not know it. If things come from some sort of nothing the universe is, and has been, always starting somewhere as nothing always exists and so as nothing beyond nature it gives eternal nature. The numbers give it infinite variety, because counting to infinity keeps finding new numbers only dividing by themselves and by one, without remainder. Infinites are composed of all the finites. Infinites with better finites are better infinites.

Chances of the ultimate and further can exist partly as things of value add up to more value than the one certain case. The divine is more than thought. Belief in God is not essential to paradise. Satisfy the person because the description that is the same as the person includes all knowledge that the person can get. This is like satisfying the knowledge.

Morals do not matter much compared to the ideal, which is found by the best truth. If paradise is had because it has the most value not because it is a reward, more people will be able to have it and this will put up its value. The aesthetics of paradise are of course limited to pleasure, and want satisfaction.

The brain could be used to extend language.

During infinite 'A' and infinite 'B' one is always ahead of the other giving a better infinite. If sometimes the less good overtakes for a while the best still has the best finites during infinity.

The ultimate is a direction that may go beyond the ultimate, in paradise or what it becomes.

The chance, which is negligible compared to infinity which makes it like certainty of the ultimate or further than ultimates in infinite quality is the chance of the ultimate or further, and the ultimate or further. The chance of an infinitely meaningful description of pleasure, provides enough for this. It also provides the description of finite values. The finites extend to infinity. The parts are intrinsically finite with an infinite description as if certain. The intrinsics and so little hold the power and the glory. Do not emphasise greatness at the expense of quality. Greatness is about quality, but it is not quality. The greatness of just infinity is neutral neither good nor bad, judging by its intrinsic, which is the same as its total description. Its description includes good and bad and neutral. If you don't specialise in the positive or a positive you have positive and negative and other choices are within it.

Positive gives a choice of advantages. Holiness does not need a God. Morals are for their advantages. This is why there are morals. Society should be better off. Morals depend on certain facts and chances, as considerations but niceness has to be certain in paradise.

Sex makes one more makeable and so less valuable since less creative and makeable by evil as well as good. Right is superior to wrong.

Holiness should be consistent with being oneself. Paradise is better than happiness.

To benefit the source of the benefit improves the benefit. The causes improve.

Complex treasure. Peace to ease. Action plus prayer. Not temptation but glory. Names of God are heights. Spiritual responsibilities bring pleasure. If God is love it is more than love as is the subject love. Development further into God continuable in paradise. Indirectness and subjects achieve more. It is wise to plan. Help and be helped in pleasure. Requirements, powers, and good things are in paradise. Share lives. Power higher than strength. Paradise is the main quality because it is high, and because it has better intrinsics. Directed progress will more likely produce paradise than progress. Better progress gives better chances of infinity, and could do more of them. Bad is not appropriate description to good, so its considerations are mostly against it causing good. Bad is mostly bad not good. Good bad is a contradiction. Christ is a source of joy because he satisfies God who is in heaven, and we are taught to do likewise. The edge of God is still God. Be sent. In paradise there is no cause to lose ones temper.

You may grow more spiritually if you cultivate your inner life. Possibly God chose love as the main thing from an infinite number of concepts, or as superior to an infinite number of concepts, so there wouldn't be an infinite number of further steps at any finite rareness. Good is better than love as an object of love, and gives meaning to love, meaning is better still as includes love and good. Pleasure progresses better than good and bad because it is the most positive intrinsic we have and advantages are all positive. I believe in God as a more than infinitely

51

valuable concept. Life need not be hard. Paradise loves good enough pleasure. Advantages give more scope of newness than good and bad by better progress. Do the best quality makeable limited by an affordable price. Intrinsic quality is closer to the title quality and its description than instrumental quality is. Knowledge of advantages is alright. There are many opinions but mankind tends to a valuable answer so that a majority is better than just any opinion. Go to paradise and your past sins will not have bad effect on you, and the morals of paradise are easy, because they have to completely satisfy the self. Love is part of positive meaning and helpful to the finites of infinity. Love the infinitely further than love.

Love main infinites. Knowledge of good and its synonyms should be the basis of wealth. Money is a power. Morals are a form of quality. Intrinsic quality is nearer the subject quality than instrumental quality. Worthwhile meaning gives point to things, and pleasure has higher meaning, giving more value, and more point. Value helps define the kind of highness. Value and pleasure are both considerations as to what to have. The more known value the better the infinite.

The self is the centre so it is right to have one's own opinion rather than any ones.

There are a number of considerations against evil causing good. One can extrapolate for unfound knowledge. Good is not appropriate to the description of evil. Advantages

52

are positive not negative so evil only has inappropriate good advantages. Whether there is a God or not, good judgements will come to the world. The best good is pleasure. In unfound knowledge good need not take bad into account so good causing good in unfound knowledge has a proper bias. All things have a chance of an infinite description but some things are particularly significant positively infinitely in description. Quality and its synonyms are advantages. Good and its synonyms is the same as quality and its synonyms. They have positive rich meaning. Meaning gives point. Emotion is rich. Paradise is the same. Anything is a subject. Pleasure can be about further than pleasure. Once one has point one can ask 'are there any unfound alternatives to point?' The subject 'an infinite number of alternatives to point' contains about an infinite number and they can be placed in order of preference if found. Better and best are more likely positive than negative, because of their advantages. Good has advantages bad disadvantages.

There is the subject "advantages and an infinite number of further steps", served by the best advantages. Quality and its synonyms does aspects of its nature. Knowledge goes to goodness, not evil. The better part of the understanding has beauty.

The highest wisdom is divine. It is up to us whether or not we lessen bad to a negligible quantity. Good and its synonyms in pleasure is a paradise. Nature is infinitely better than bad is because good and its synonyms progress better, and this is all in its description. Bad getting worse lessens. With bad causing good one has to take. The disadvantages degree from the advantages degree. With good causing good one can sometimes add a degree of good. To the second good.

The joy of Christ is the strength, beauty, and glory of the Christian. Having paradise is moral. The sinner should go there. Paradise is meant for us, if there is a good God. We haven't had it before, except for a few people, because God is limited by nature if there is a God. This is why there is evil. Studying the few people who claim to be in paradise may cause many in paradise. There is nothing further than steps that may be endless, doable at present as a subject, or a no maximum beyond infinity.

Wonderfulness all the time is more wonderful, than for a few moments. Be noble and heavenly, have good enough improvement. This will serve best. Transcend yourself, if you can. This is light, love is free and not necessary in paradise. Moral perfection is not needed in paradise. It is too difficult. Forgiveness does not need belief in God. Man can forgive man. Morals fit human nature, only without bad in a just good world, and being able to be just good is a moral opinion or right of man. Good serves infinity. The chance of an infinite God is a negligible chance, so it is as if certain. It's as if there was a God, at least. Religion gives proper moral considerations that are not just reason without divine revelation.

Answering is endless but better throughout infinity is got by keeping each policy a long time. An infinite number of them is still done.

It is favourable and wonderful that good and its direction further is the answer to life.

Nature is a wonder, including the spirit, soul, or mind. If there is an afterlife it is part of nature. God is part of nature. Transcendence is only in nature. The universe was created to contribute to progress or better than progress. The size of the universe is a wonder seek the divine. Faith makes one wise. The subject good infinity includes any number of infinites of infinites. Infinite evil may be an infinitely small proportion, or very small finite proportion. Lessening evil exceptions could add up to lessening intrinsic evil in an infinite time.

Qualities give a variety of infinites. Infinite space is in the description. Intrinsic infinite space might be got by expansion during an infinite time and this gives a better infinite than description. There is no maximum to the universes completed infinity. The quality direction is a wondrous treasure. Perfection is steps. Infinity is steps. Paradise is steps. Paradise is the available next step. Advantages are more than one step. An infinite number of steps. Further than love in a love direction is in the description of love.

Having a good, if it means avoiding a bad is twice the advantage. Bad is a synonym of wrong and this means it may be included in wrong, or shares much of the description of wrong. Appropriateness of good to good probably has considerations of value. A world of just bad would not progress unless to good, because it would have no advantages. Selected advantages help with ones aims. Good with good is appropriate. Bad with good in its description has partial appropriateness. Infinite love is infinitely valuable. Improve upon staying okay. God in man's image is part of God. All good can be holy good. Paradise becomes amazing good. Height but not just any kind of height can enable paradise. Paradise is infinitely more valuable than non-paradise. The difference in description grows to infinity. Just good is nearer perfection. A paradise utopia is further good, more limiting except perhaps by better progress. Punishment is an evil, for good effect. For faith there is quality and its synonyms taken further and infinitely.

Holiness is included. Comfort man's mortality with an immortal grace. Bad is described most appropriately as bad not a form of good. Non-paradise is wrong. Wrong goes because progress causes better. Cause and effect does not just cause events whether right of wrong but we care about right and good. Considerations progress more in favour of good than bad with good and the disadvantages of bad should tend to lessen. Good is parts of good. The heart can be in keeping with thought, and naturalness high, advantage constant, marvels of technology will come, better progress and more good, by putting resources into specifically how, and happiness will flourish. People are significant. The self can be made more good and is great. Have a fantastic future. We are part of possibly infinite time and the chance is negligible. So it is as if certain. Want satisfactions is an intrinsic good and so suited to paradise, where it is constant. If courage is a virtue it is a lesser virtue and not needed in the heights. Intrinsic quality and its synonyms, for example intrinsic good and intrinsic holiness, are pleasures. Intrinsic value is more true of value than instrumental value as a cause which is indirect. Love heightens beauty.

 Holiness is basic to its many further steps past holiness with a chance of an infinite number of steps at any finite rareness of concept in a possibly infinite description. The possibility is negligible compared to infinity and so it is as if certain. The best quality and synonyms are holy. Holy love is part of holy pleasure, not holy pleasure part of holy love, perhaps. Temptation is replaced by want satisfaction. Progress in pleasure and its synonyms in general is the best way to find new parts of the main subjects.

Paradise is needed partly because the brain hasn't had time enough to adapt to its new parts. Man is going against himself. The person's basic nature which is his name should be fitted. In animals this fit helped survival in evolution. Fitting the person puts all in fit in the person. Ethics can be high and spiritual. So religion is good. Good spreads when it can. Man should learn worthwhile things about himself and for himself. Consistency and order are helpful, serving good.

Existences and their interconnections in law have a unity of nature and single name 'existence.' Paradise is part of this. The universe is perhaps the best practical universe, or alternative to best in unfound concepts. Any concept is an infinite subject with a chance that is negligible compared to infinity so it is as is certain, and has a chance of infinity beyond infinity.

The atomic cannot do all our things. It is neither intrinsically good not bad but neutral in itself. It has no meaning in itself, like sensory vision or sound. It is a giant neutral alien. Thought that isn't emotion is dead. The neutralness of the atomic frees mankind to do anything it wants. Faith doesn't need proof of God and doesn't need a God. Knowing the immoral to avoid it is bad for good. Morals should not be a burden. Depression and anxiety are ended by going to paradise. Better relationships and more positive accomplishments are advantages. Positive psychology is a step towards paradise. Positiveness helps life in general because postiveness is advantages. Postiveness produces more thought of right, I expect. Paradise being positive is nearer just good than instrumental good. Some people are in paradise. Religion is only a free to refuse option as part of a manmade paradise, but good relationships between people is required if not Christian love. Hedonism, the morals stating pleasure is the answer, can be added to other morals, in paradise. May pleasure bless you.

Note book 2

A chance of an infinite description has a chance of an infinite number of considerations adding up to its value. The chance being negligible so it is as if certain. A finite frequency of considerations in an infinite description gives an infinite number of value considerations.

Positive point has meaning and advantages. Love of quality and it synonyms has positive point. One can go infinitely further, in subject. This is better. This is personified for further value. Each step beyond a concept is as if infinite, creating better and better infinites, or unfound alternative to better, or further and further in a desirable direction. An infinite subject at any finite proportion of infinite worth has infinite worth. The subject is about a chance of infinity and the chance being negligible gives as if certain infinity. The ultimate has a chance of being finite and surpassed or infinite and surpassed. The subjects are composed of differentiating infinites, which as if add, because everything has a chance of an infinite description. The ultimate has a chance of an infinite number of steps further in unfound concepts, which for an ultimate of infinity can give a more than infinitely valuable subject. The average steps could be infinite. This has a chance. Everything is a chance. There are no absolute infinite certainties.

Depth produces more height. Truth is not all good. Ease helps more than struggle. Want satisfaction is creative as well as needs. Do not overcome part of the self for virtue.

This has bad care and unquietness. Make pleasure of virtues. Self-love can help happiness. Have love in maintaining and expressing the self. Intrinsic positiveness is real positiveness. Positive value is value. Paradise is a possibility so you can want it. Infinite quality has infinite advantages. Be saved from a base, mad mixture of good and bad experience. The amount of good between exceptions of bad being more, more good is created by exceptions of bad. More good is also created by good. Height is approximately basic. To improvement, love life or like life.

Advantages tend to have other advantages. They have positive meaning, and point. The attraction in wanted pleasure has point and value which extends infinitely. Be pure and good. Be morally pure, and justified and morally at home. The mind has a wonderful potential. If everyone caused right instead of wrong there would be no wrong. Bad progresses to less bad, good to more good, because progress is positive, concerned with advantages. Alternatively bad increases to cause more good.

Mathematically a finite chance of infinity equals a certain infinity. The description of pleasure may be infinite. Bad creating good is creating the opposite of its nature. This is far enough away not to be natural to the nature of bad. It cannot cause enough good. Good causing good is the answer. Bad has no advantages of its own only good aspects. The infinite description of pleasure is the same thing as pleasure. If it is chance it evaluates at certain infinity. Wellbeing is incomplete without satisfying pleasure all the time. Emphasising bad makes it definitely too bad but emphasising good does not make it too good. If pleasure is as if infinite and describes beyond pleasure in its direction it is important. Pleasure and its synonyms and want satisfaction constitute paradise, or a utopia. Holiness only requires aspects one can believe in. The chance of infinity is not so poor it reduces infinity infinitely to finite value. Good does greater in quantities than the quantities of rare bad during infinity, although they are both infinite. The good infinite is greater. Rare bad still adds up to infinitely less during infinity by less making and less progress described. The finite advantages add to infinity. Would be bads that aren't bad have more scope than bad. Scope by progress has advantages into the unknown. Continuous contribution to nature contributes more than the ultimate. If quality or pleasure has an infinite description it has an infinite number of infinite descriptions. Only one is needed to describe infinitely an infinite number of steps further than perfection or infinitely past the ultimate. This one infinite description has an infinite number of infinite descriptions. God did not tell us about infinitely further than perfection partly because a thousand years is almost no time at all compared to eternity.

Multiply more good than bad by infinity and one gets infinite bad, infinite good and infinitely more good than bad. You multiply by infinity because of the chance of an infinite description. Have justice, joy and peace in goodness and further. Have quality planning in pleasure. Have great and immaculate bliss. If inevitability exists existence exists. Existence is what we have got. Paradise is part of existence. Increase the riches within. Paradise has advantages and an infinite number of steps further than advantages in its direction as a subject. There is the subject better and past paradise or past niceness and satisfaction in paradise. This is to be blessed. This is the greatest glory except there are an infinite number of steps beyond glory in subject. It perhaps takes God an infinite time to create things. But steps have an infinite superseding. There are possibly and in subject an infinite number of steps past infinity, better or alternative to better. This may be eternity.

Infinity is nothing without quality or something to give it point. Quality gives infinitely further than itself. Pleasure and satisfaction is the highest available quality apart from taking into account the great subjects. It has a chance of an infinite description including great subjects passing infinity. Pleasure can have more quality by choice from a selection. More intrinsic quality has a better infinity. Have faith in advantages and further. The world has been allowed. Glorify the great subjects. Bad is unnatural.

The chance of pleasure doing infinitely better than the ultimate of progress is better than the chance it is less good or less satisfactory than that ultimate or that it is that ultimate. Also, paradise does the subject an infinite number of steps further than pleasure better than non-paradise.

Pleasure is our best thing for describing the unknown, leaving out bad. Good goes to height. Height can have more meaning. There are probably lots of ways of dividing value up. The subject possibly further than pleasure is done by the subjects possibility, further than, and pleasure. It could be the actual thing, but any finite step would barely improve description. Indirect description is less relevant. Taking larger pieces of description would compensate and be still an infinite amount. Nature works like red and blue making purple, not exactly as conceived, and not as mathematics entirely. All available answers to life are either good and bad or good. There is the chance of knowledge going so much further in conception. We live in a wonderful world. Progress rather than searching in knowledge is the answer because its things go beyond present conception and get better.

If chances of infinity don't always equal certainty of infinity they do in evaluation. Infinite value has infinite variety, because pure repetition does not differentiate, so does not add up. Good and further always belongs to God, therefore is very great. Quality in pleasure is two goods. This makes three positives. This makes four worthwhile things. Proper pleasure has more than attraction it has positive meaning. Right has positive meaning. Pureness is an example. The subject infinitely further than the satisfactory ultimate in unfound concepts or phenomena is an example. Right is justified by chance. Ending wrong, by quitting action, is acceptable. The

63

finites during infinity can add, or subtract. Different phenomena are partly separate from each other so bad is partly separate from any good it causes and needs to be partly estimated separately. Want satisfaction has a complex brain effect. This should be taken into account to help determine wants or we do not suit our brains well enough. We should aim at good brain quality use. Christ did not suffer to pay for our sins. Justice does not need punishment but progress, and other methods, such as a good or better upbringing. Friendship is high. A life of the atomic senses and feelings from them is not all.

The supernatural is not infinitely far off. Bad for good will have to go for Christ to reign. Repentance is not so important as height, or paradise. Nourish with pleasant food. A quality paradise excels. Reality is that pleasure and want satisfaction, and further in subject is the answer to life. Quality is riches of mind, nobleness, moral behaviour, peace, good ability, pleasure, good management, happiness, wellbeing, light, holiness, beauty, incentive selective, satisfaction, sufficient answering of problems, right not wrong, good in the arts, classicalness and usefulness, wider than economics, antiques, comfort, attraction, manners, the precious, good environment, parties celebrating, The National Trust, positive psychology, conservation, wonder, the worthwhile, progress, what you do best, successful living, blessedness, good education, positive parenting, satisfaction, golden ages, good potential and so on.

Better quality has a chance of infinitely better description. The finites during all infinity tending to better, possibly. Because positive value doesn't take from value it is positive. Quality of knowledge is largely the subject quality. Answers to life are part of good or part of good and bad, or the answer is good or good and bad. Opinions are chances of good and good and bad. Logic is not the basis of nature but the reasonableness of red and blue making purple, in experience. Future development of culture could be glorious. Right is in favour of good and quality partly because they are synonyms of right. All three are positives. The proper knowledge will create paradise. A manmade paradise would be nearer to God. A world of just good magnifies good. Good compared to good and bad need only be better on average times the number of cases which is the total value. The average can include less valuable cases than good and bad. We should compare two cases of good to one bad and to one good, in bad for good.

Bad should be uncommon. Good quality pleasure and synonyms are the best things available to deal with the subjects past ultimate things and perfection. Pamper yourself. Open you heart. If God is perfect or better than perfect in unfound concepts knowledge benefits, but not knowledge of evil. Knowledge of God is imperfect but good. Paradise should be the best quality and synonyms, including serving the great subjects. More scope of more newnesses can be got by better progress or further than progress. Most considerations are in favour of good

(which is positive) and against bad simply because good
has advantages bad disadvantages. More bad for less bad
should end, sooner or later. The earth must go up.
Progress may go to the largely unknown beforehand again
and again. The world builds on the past, extends and
limits again and again. Paradise might visit, ending bad
and increasing good. The value of pleasure is not just
appeal. It included meaning. A heaven is at hand. Part of
a growth towards fuller union with God. Paradise is got
by directing progress and development, and by
appreciating intrinsic qualities or by more quality than
just happiness by height, and by making pleasure and
want satisfaction. Pleasure assists health and wellbeing
and sometimes gives spiritual nourishment, and improves
upon nastiness and neutralness. The best forces available
should shape your life. Be good wholesome and sound.
Be happy in a positive mind-set. A good cost is part of
quality. Morals are part of quality. Excellence is part of
quality, good ability also. Potential quality is a part. A
good home is part of quality. The legacy of pleasure is
part of quality. Good qualities, are not just a matter of
value I believe. Holiness for example. With heart and
soul, trust and religious faith, endeavour and benefit. Be
relaxed and at ease, with better and hope of still better.
Have good nourishment for the mind, a light to itself. A
constant blessing. God's hand at work, mysticism.
Beauty with attraction and height upon height. The heart
is the well-spring of life (prov. 4.23). Be kind to each
other and to yourself. Sooner or later paradise will enter
the transcendent for those that want it. All shall be well.

The description of the absolute is in things. In describing a thing one can say 'other things are so and so' and describe the rest of nature. I hope heart, body and soul will fill with joy. Goodness and its synonyms being proper are the reality. Bad is false. As reality, good and its synonyms are the truth. The spirit should need the body and mind. The atomic environment in experience is part of the self. One is like a small world. Height for pleasure. Heightened perception may come. Our knowing of things brings life about all things.

If you go partly beyond the atomic you can be believed mad, although it is more your own mind. More opportunity in the scope of good and quality comes from emphasising a knowledge of good and quality, without bad. Having a job you like is not only possible but reasonable. Education allows higher worth.

Pleasure and want satisfaction soothe the self and have harmony with the self. We need to take an infinite number of steps by progress in an infinite time by any finite quantity during, because one cannot find the best in a non-ending sequence, and there is always further. Progress increases ability to answer. Good is better and better at ability. The opposites of good and bad don't attract themselves together. Searching instead of doing answers for a while will not get one further if there is still infinite time. Good probably describes bad by would be bads so bad isn't needed. We are very young compared with eternity. An infinite number of universes have been possibly created before this one. People should think up great good to do. Love is higher and more valuable than liking. Infinite love is possibly intrinsic not just description. Glory is higher than love, or is part of love and its appropriate description. The description adds to love, although it is not intrinsic love only descriptive good love. The subject 'an infinite number of steps beyond love' is more valuable than love. This makes its infinity partly there by aspects of its nature, not the finites of infinity but infinity itself. Steps and beyond infinity are part of the description of infinity because there are an infinite number of them. The subject has a chance of an infinite description of worthwhile things and the chance is negligible compared to infinity. The description is the same as the thing described, so description exists. If there is infinite goodness and pleasure the subject infinite goodness and pleasure has infinite value because the subject cannot lessen infinite reality to finite reality as this is an infinite step, which is too big, and a finite is the next quantity below infinity. For infinite value the subject would be infinitely big but an infinitely small fraction gives infinite value as it is infinite or one or any finite value averaging infinity. The chance of infinite good and pleasure or further is a negligible chance compared to infinity. There is glory or further in the good and truth. Bad for good has to be in favour of its good in spite of bad whereas good is just good so unfound knowledge is more in favour of just good. Just good only has considerations in favour of it. Considerations against would show bad to be there. But intrinsic good is just observation. The description of good includes bad but is not appropriate description, bad being the opposite of good. More pleasure available will heighten the worship of God. Enough proper pleasure could end nastiness, also with want satisfaction.

An infinity of infinites is in an infinity and infinite number of things can be described infinitely in an infinite description. Quality raised is pleasure. The right morals take one towards paradise. The cross transformed isn't a bad cross. The full description of love is the totality of nature but the appropriateness of description gives a distinction from other things. One can say with anything 'further things are there' and indicate the rest of nature in describing a thing. The description also includes what isn't in existence, but to describe it gives it some existence. The description is the same as the thing described so is there. There are any number of would be bads higher than each bad but one should not know bads to raise them. Computers in the neutralness of the atomic do mathematical would bees. There are other would bees. Stronger pleasures in paradise could sometimes be used as incentives to lesser pleasures. Any pleasure has a chance of an infinite number of good things in its more appropriate description. Different pleasures give differentiating infinites so infinite plus infinite equals more than just infinity. They have separate existence. The finites in infinites may be added together in whole infinites giving greater infinites, by more during their infinity. Advantages are all positive, and any great aim is best done with advantages added to it. Further value and advantages give the best chances of beyond since may be part of the way to better and may be a direction, or have further.

Glory is the aim of this book. Proper pleasure can be Godly, and its description includes the whole of existence and non-existence. In describing anything one can say 'other things exist' and indicate the rest of things, and the description if the same as the thing described so is there. Eternity is in that description, but hell is not appropriate enough description. Scope and selected advantages, for example ability, are better for the unknown, doing better progress than bad, and being better. The unknown has the best chances improved upon if the good unknown because it already has something. An infinite number of steps further than better in a better direction is in the subject and description of better, and has chances of infinity. Paradise is better and further than better. Infinitely further than paradise in a paradise direction is a subject done in paradise and is better for things from the unknown. Going infinitely beyond quality and all its synonyms are subjects done in paradise. Scope and selected advantages for the unknown become secondary to infinitely further, as subjects in paradise. One does the best things but the most value is got by the best average times number of things. There are more good things than good.

We satisfy wants instead of satisfying wants that fit the complexity of the brain so civilisation has gone wrong. The brain complexity could give stronger and more natural want satisfaction and give more to take into account, and a more positive life. At present not want and lesser wants appear after want satisfaction because of bad brain fit.

Perfection goes from chance to certainty. Good is infinite but further than good in a good direction gives better during infinity and a better quality infinity. Infinity adds more meaning than the finite, or further than meaning in a meaning direction. Leave wrong, do the infinites in pleasure or good, for further infinite value. Good for example does the description of its aspects but each aspect has its own appropriateness of description, more there, if the aspect is intrinsic. The description is the same as the intrinsic described. Some people are in paradise. We should learn from them.

Note book 3

Select and create methods of being properly just nice and satisfied. Repetition, height, intrinsic quality, blends, new combinations, formula, holiness, beauty, wonder, kinds of joy, desire, music, these are some. Part ways can sometimes be taken all the way by complete ways. Love, enchantment, computer complexity. Finding by association and attraction, intrinsic positiveness, more gladness, enough positive meaning, selected education, intrinsic treasure, these are some others. Perhaps utopia first, then paradise. Stick to pleasure and want satisfaction by its nature. Personified good is a good spirit. More positive good gives a gain. An alternative to bad for good effect is less good in good for more good. Endless answering of answers is more valuable as a chance than finite answering. Increasing good and lessening bad may go to paradise. Pleasure is a good. Freedom is in degrees. Be justified. Better during infinity is a better infinity, during infinity can be composed of infinites but these are composed of finites. You cannot add finite to infinity for more than infinity but you can add finite to finite during an infinity of finites.

During an infinity of finites it is always finite. God can be finite and infinite. Chances are in the process of becoming more and more certainties and realised concepts. Their description adds up to love and everything else. Everything is in the description of each thing because one can say 'further things exist' and give all, when describing a thing. Positive meaning is better than love and includes love, in more than an infinite number of descriptive steps with no maximum and bad negligible in comparison.

Don't live a hard life. Morals, also, are imperfect, since opinion. If you don't do all your moral opinion you are forgiven, because punishment is a nastiness not believed in by paradise. Fictional bads that appear real are really bad. For example saying 'he's murdered' is the same true or false so contains the nature of real bad. Paradise grows upwards and outwards. Proper pleasure and want satisfaction constitute part of the kingdom of heaven. Steps beyond these in their direction or at an angle are to us only a chance, description and subject. Ideal at more than an infinite number of steps further. Pleasure and want satisfaction is a paradise. Gods future and further include the main parts of the concept of God. The right moral will help get you to paradise. Ability is also needed. Quality improves ability. Humanise more not less. Paradises nature is mostly not in the bible. Would be bads increase the scope of good. Bad has a chance of satisfactory unknown natures, but good has a better chance of satisfactory unknown natures. Infinite good and infinite bad contain such, but infinite bad may have lesser finites during infinity. Finites exist throughout infinity. Free people choose morals.

Paradise has its own aesthetics.

Satisfactory new things have to have positive meaning or something to take its place, as a content or accompaniment, or something to take the place of these. Something new to take the place of satisfactory may also be found. Such things need to be better or something to take the place of the better. An infinite number of steps beyond quality in a quality direction has a chance of an infinite number of steps further than better. This is a subject.

For the word infinite do a small infinity and then one really has infinity. It is without end, yet complete. Positive thinking can increase joy, and has other advantages. There is no punishment in paradise and we are told in the bible to do on earth as in heaven. Good in the unknown has a chance of an infinite description, and so is taken as infinite. The no maximum has a chance of going further than all alternatives. Follow your dreams. Quality adds being to the thing of quality to have that quality. Description adds that being. This multiplies its nature in God. Pleasure is an intrinsic quality and intrinsic good. Chances of infinity can be very small and still negligible compared to infinity so as if the position was certain. Fictional evil is not paradisiacal. Pleasure and satisfaction are the aesthetes of paradise. Hedonism should be tempered by other morals, without bad for good. Each want satisfying. Pleasure being positive has a chance of an infinite positive appropriate description giving infinite value. Each description differentiates, so adds to more than infinite value.

Infinite steps further than good in a good direction or near to it, gives better infinites in description, and chance or alternatives to better infinites.

Wrong is more than right so bad for good is more bad than good in unfound knowledge. Bad to lessen bad more than it increases it does not have this disadvantage. Infinite good beats infinite bad in differentiating infinites, that add more and by greater finites during infinity. Good is the answer and synonyms, and infinitely further. Both are done because the lesser serves the greater, and adds to great subjects. Live with depth. This gives significance and more. If one in a thousand people are in paradise that is several million people. The disadvantages in various moral opinions are evils for good. Just pleasure and want satisfaction avoid these morals, because they are just good, and have morals of their own. The possibility negligible compared to infinity. Say a thing is real, God for example, and the reality possibilities have an infinite description. The chance being negligible compared to infinity. The chance of infinity being negligible means infinity is as if certain. The same applies to the chance of no maximum. Infinity alone would be a maximum. At a finite fraction of infinite description of pleasure an infinite number of advantages can be found. Although considerations in favour of good and bad and just good can be taken as both infinite because good need not take bad into account, the proportion during infinity gains in favour of good. In an infinite description there is an infinite number of differentiating infinites but there is still more if the description of another thing is added. Do progress into paradise. Paradise is higher and more satisfying the happiness.

Evil causing good is less appropriate to good than good giving a less appropriate chance of an infinite description. Paradise is a service of nature.

In a way infinity is a no maximum. Proper pleasure that satisfies want is the answer, which does greater. Knowing the world is knowing the self. It is the self which is holy. In the description of better is the chance of an infinite, or no maximum not infinity number of steps beyond better in a better direction in unfound concepts. In present language these concepts would take more and more language to put each one. The truth appears to be mostly true wrongs. The truth which is the answer is a very small proportion of the truth. There is answering and progressing forever, in a chance negligible compared to infinity. An infinite number of finites compose infinity. The finites are always there so it is complete. It would not be infinite if it was not complete.

There is a more appropriate description and also a description of anything that includes all nature which goes to very small appropriateness, at the least, not none. Appropriateness to the self is more satisfying then just going beyond and can still go beyond by progress within satisfaction. Just going beyond is largely bad due to inappropriateness. Progressing at home and contributing to nature for longer during the one answer or set of

76

answers gives better finites to your possible infinity. I believe paradise can be, or is, the most appropriate and satisfying answer available and it can do the great subjects. One has to deny oneself the intrinsic to do an instrumental aim, except when the two are the same. This gives delayed satisfaction and is part of non-paradise.

An infinite number of differentiating infinites is not the limit because that can be differentiated from. Each step has a better infinite, and chance of no maximum better than the step before. Let the available divine be in pleasure, adding infinite value and more to the great subjects. Pleasure and would be other in pleasure includes all things possibly. There are more would bees than actualities. To know the world is to know the self but other people and one's self are holy and important. Any positive knowledge in paradise is worthwhile for the great subjects as we don't entirely know what will go into the subjects and help. For example, the finite is an infinitely small proportion to infinity but a finite fraction of infinity is infinite. Ideas about paradise don't need proof. Intrinsic value is pure value. Niceness and its meanings are different from pure value but yet have it. The causes of paradise can include some bad as long as this goes. Paradise should then last by niceness and satisfaction creating niceness and satisfaction and by enough width of creativity in niceness and other means for avoiding bad. Right is one of these. Being angelic another. The right kind of height is a great help. The morals of paradise must be nice and satisfying so they are easy. Selection of good means knowing bad and is not a right method.

Why hasn't modern man risen more? What could be done about it? Good is priceless. Right knowledge is one requirement. Good is better than good and bad and paradise is high good. Good has more advantages than bad. Perhaps because good and advantages are both positive. Paradise is also positive, and part of good. Positive means it can gain. Make life more meaningful. Advantages can be added to the unknown that becomes known. The unknown should be unknown pleasure, because if good and bad are infinite, pleasure as a fraction is infinite.

Normalness and naturalness of brain is part of the answer. This is because the brain has had millions of years of progress so that the total combinations of parts is enormous. The combinations are so complicated they are of unknown quality. But we satisfy want without taking the complexity of the brain into account, which would give different want. This means judging brain combinations.

The brain is best natural since the past was natural. Natural is easy. It is the most true life.

Paradise is by God's right hand. Other good besides pleasure can be in pleasure. Softness rather than hardness. Naturalness may produce paradise, because it is natural to want pleasure with satisfaction. Feel high with God or Christ. The ordinary will be transformed, with or without religion.

The chance of an infinite number of steps beyond perfection in a perfection direction may be very small but any chance compared to infinity is negligible. Each step gives a better infinity to have a chance of. The chance of infinite further steps has an infinite of a high order, giving an infinitely better infinite. This is in the appropriate description of the positive not the negative.

If description is infinite there is always a better answer to life. The negligible chance means this is as if it was certain.

Quality is related to effectiveness. Statistical method is used. Excellence is attempted.

Excellence or holiness is a step beyond just pleasure. This is infinite by chance and subject of an infinite description. There infinity is positive or further than positive in a positive direction, or maybe other acceptable nature, infinitely further of no maximum. Bad will make lesser finites during infinity, infinity being composed of finites, and no maximum is composed if infinites. So is composed of finites also. In naturalness ease and sensuality are more. Feminine aspects of the self are needed. The mystical is a potential in every person. The atomic known in the mind has quality and evil, but the atomic itself is neutral. Make life, deep and fascinating.

During infinity is always finite so infinity can do better finites. If anything in knowledge stops at proof of an answer to life this really has a very small chance it isn't proof and the best chances are with the infinitely further. The ideal if found is probably an advantage, and positive, or more positive than negative. Better is more positive. We haven't found any alternatives to good and bad because alternatives are small fractions of infinity (yet are infinite,) or because they are distant from our nature.

Blending plainness or other source produced richness which had positive and negative meanings. Emotion is a richness and this is the source of good and bad. Perhaps bad was not avoided because the animals had an exception with their paradise nature. Man has extended this because his more recent brain parts haven't had time to completely fit his other parts. The mind as well as the atomic caused evolution. Difficulty which can perhaps be unconscious may have freed us from the rule of instinct, but this causes bad. The aliens allowed us to be partly bad because they are not sure which best suits our natures, paradise or non-paradise.

Peace encourages harmony, and naturalness, and God. Goodness has little cause to lie. Find personal light. Be yourself clearly. This gives good fit. Good thoughts heighten. Gain a higher self-worth. Care for yourself. Be intimate. We are already high but could be higher. Use positive language. Focus on pleasure when it gives satisfaction. Positive emotion make a better use of time and power and the power of good increases good in the self and care for others. You are precious. Human nature has power. An open heart can allow love. Release yourself in prayer. Stretch your mind. Have priorities, and give time to them. Learn, organise, grow and get better. Sing or dance. Take your time. Travel light. Change into part of paradise. Celebrate faith. Pleasure causing pleasure. Have a Christian's guide to happiness. How to make children happy. Be relaxed at all times. Give a good surprise. Be admirable. Live your bliss. Go in for the feel good factor. Grow though joy. Cost benefit analysis. Friendship. Spiritual gardening. Better surroundings. Help with our dreams. Pleasure in history. Learning from high class society in history. Global quality. Operations and quality management. Continuous quality improvement. Quality of life. The beatitudes of the bible. Spirit and beauty. The richness within. Flower gardens. Joy in just living. Flowers with love. High scent. Recreation and leisure. Learning from summer. A home a paradise. Achievement. Power freedom and grace. Joy in Jesus. Ethics and excellence. Work with passion. Fulfilling worth. Working from the heart. Enchanting business. How to get the best out of everything. God's treasury. High and selected entertainment. Spiritual gifts. Sensuous glory. Birthday and Christmas parties. Celebrating the seasons of life. The sublime. Laid back joy. Hedonism. Blissed out. Euphoric and empyrean. Better than words can say. Good quality antiques. Learning from non-Christian religions. Romances and comedies. Classical literary criticism. Tourism and holidays. Churches. Cheering words. A psychic pathway to joy. Pleasure and desire. More precious things than gold. The happy countryman. Joy in various good things. Health within capacity. How to get what you want out of life. A history of heaven as we have conceived it. Enjoying eating and drinking. High musicals and opera.

The soul loves the truth.

Note book 4

The holy spirit. A modern mystic's way. Christian themes in contemporary poets. Embracing a theology of wonder. Aspects of Christmas copied for always. Passion and society. Evaluation. Safety games and exercises. Choice desire and the will of God. Positive pupil management and motivation. Spiritual mothering. Growing through encouragement. Giving your child a better start. Positive parenting. Values education and the adult. The golden age of childhood. Enjoyment and the activity of mind. Church dogmatics knowing with the heart. Brilliant memory.

Social wellbeing.

Art in golden ages. Art and understanding. The aesthetic appreciation of nature. Aesthetics and politics. The aesthetics of computing. The smile of love. The meanings of love. Family values – to love is to be happy with.

Celebrating marriage. Spiritual friendship. The art of loving food as presents. Cooking for celebrations. Entertaining with great dishes of the world. God's good fruit of the spirit. Wisdom. Motivation. Romancing the ordinary. Music of the heart. Selected social history. The virtues of the courtesans. Nudes and glamour, women and beauty. Plants with impact. A love affair with jewellery. Gift books. Silver and gold objects. The divine enchantment. Natural law and natural rights. The ascent of man. Significance. A good new age. The pearl of great price. The pursuit of beauty. Finding divine inspiration. The crown of life.

A temple of heaven. The glory of God's grace. How to enjoy your retirement. An ethical analysis of Christian love. The beauty of Jesus. Flourish.

How to be green.

A passion for holiness.

Love creates positive experiences. Do joy plus realisation. Wellbeing accompanies joy. Have an inner balance, by good. If your days are good I expect your dreams at night are good.

One cannot go any further than the negligible chance and subject of concepts or being at no maximum further than no maximum. Beyond good is to more and more satisfying or alternative to satisfying. For example more and more justified in aim. The same proportion of good and bad approximately during all infinity gains an ever increasing difference of good compared to bad. The main subject and chances are done in pleasure for further point.

Collect ways of improving wants. Positive thinking is better thinking. Pleasure is more positive. Positiveness can improve emotional intelligence.

Positiveness is better at progress. Method can improve achievement. Quality can improve continuously.

Anchor heaven's light on earth. Drugs for quality not just health. Have high family values.

Learn to do better. Selected pleasure from pleasure is better.

Benefit society rather than individuals, even if not most of society. Better is better than normalness. Progress from normalness to quality and its synonyms.

Add infinite advantages to the new. Nothing is completely different. All nature is related and in the description of each thing, because it is in nature. The supernatural is in nature. The principle of law is followed by religion which is followed by the aim of paradise on earth.

The chance of God is infinitely valuable because the chance of an infinite God is negligible compared to infinity. In usual mathematics a finite chance of infinity equals a certainty of infinity.

The description of a good thing is in other good things but not so much there. This applies throughout the description and so is taken as infinite differences.

The truth directs freedom.

Properness is perhaps strengthened in paradise, likewise holiness. Morals are easy since pleasant and satisfying.

The truth is the main truth, first and foremost. This states that good is worthwhile and its direction further than good, has point. This is true even if it is chance. Pleasure is good.

Value or further or positive direction description, being there because it is the same as the thing described, added to nature throughout its duration and size has more point than the ultimate best. If the answer is progress then progress is the ultimate not just the way to the ultimate. Good gives a better chance than bad of answerings, and pleasure is high good. Answering may keep getting better and be generally good so answers generally contribute. The chance of endless answering and a maximum to it or not, beyond infinity, is perhaps the main answer.

Safety is in the positive description. Paradise is light not heavy. Ordered not chaotic. Light hearted not cold. Soft and clean.

Have style and substance. Beauty and holiness.

Dynamics of human life with pleasure.

Have pleasure with quality and want satisfaction.

With good and bad for causing good the proportion of bad could get worse while the quantity of good minus bad gets more. This cannot, however, quite reach a proportion half bad half good, where good minus bad is nothing. For example, with equal degrees of bad and good, one bad with two good gives one good 18 bad 20 good give two good but is a worse proportion.

Good bad is a contradiction. This probably means bad cannot cause enough good to ever be good.

Pleasure goes beyond infinity because infinity goes beyond infinity, with a chance and subject of an infinite number of further steps at any finite rareness or not of concepts.

Aim at a deep and lasting fulfilment.

Suffering with ignorance is based on fake ideas of reality, according to Buddhism.

An infinite description perhaps goes past infinity in reasonable knowledge.

Paradise is pure good but niceness, want satisfaction and opinion, which is free to differ. Wants are within reason, and so limited.

Eternity contains an infinite number of further steps but has no beginning as well, and perhaps goes beyond infinity.

Morals are advantages.

If infinite descriptions get less appropriateness into infinity take bigger and bigger sections for the same value so the value is still infinite, because there is an infinite number of these sections.

The soul is a higher concept than the mind. Religion heightens.

Have a more humanised culture. Be enchanted. Be easy not attempting control. Aim to become carefree. Have a rich, useful imagination to the mind and realities of the mind need not be always be about the atomic. Dreams are mental realities. Different phenomena with their own and truth behaviour. There are alternative ways of feeling atomic things, more good ways. Our language cannot contain many feelings, because one cannot explain their meanings adequately, atomically.

Freedom is better than force and paradise better than freedom.

Be better than staying okay.

Pleasures should give want satisfaction, quality, height and more positive meaning. These are better if they have more size. Anyone is allowed proper paradise because it is proper. Paradise doesn't need a Christ to prepare a place for us. God forgives without having needed a payment in bad, by Christ on the cross because paradise doesn't believe in bad for good.

Different opinions from one's own should be allowed to give different lives because of freedom, and only opinion can say which is the best opinion, although judgement is open to science.

Take your time and travel light.

Two goods replace bad for good, one instead of the bad one instead of the good.

Considerations care more in favour of good than bad for good in that good progresses better than bad and so finds more points in favour. Considerations in favour are all good against all bad. Progress increases good more than bad or lessens bad and increases good. It can depend on intention. In short considerations are against bad because it is bad and in favour of good because it is good, so are against bad to cause good.

Worthwhile things extended to infinity and further are served by pleasure without knowing completely by what. This also has a chance of an infinite description.

There is no conflict with bad. It is answered. Moral chance is better than nothing, and there is the chance and subject of an infinite number of steps further than morals. This is infinitely better. Paradise will come from the study of paradise.

The chance of an infinite description of anything gives a chance in that description of an infinite number of steps past anything. The chances are negligible compared to infinity. The steps past can give better infinites by that which is during the infinities. A finite chance is a fraction times infinity over one, equals infinity by simple normal mathematics. The finite goes into infinity an infinite number of times. The finites extend to infinity and the finites of more than one infinity can add together during infinity. This can be better. Differentiating infinities add to more than infinity because they must differentiate somewhere. If they don't differentiate more than one infinite equals the same as infinite. Description gives a chance of pleasure value extending past infinity by adding the parts of description, since these have infinite differentiating value, each with an infinite description. The feelings of the meaning of the word infinity is a small infinity. That small infinity is the big one. Endless answering is improved upon by endless beyond answering beyond steps and beyond infinity, in the chance of description and as a subject. Also in the chance of infinite time. The description is the same as the thing described so it is as good as there. The description in pleasure without nastiness in description, although incomplete adds up to the thing described a number of times, and has a chance of infinite size. Nastiness isn't appropriate, but the description must total at good if the thing described is good because they are the same thing.

There is a chance of an infinite difference between good and bad in the descriptions of pleasure. The good being more appropriate than the bad adds up to pleasure.

Pleasure is intrinsically good. It is desirable because it has part of positive intrinsic advantage.

Quality has positive meaning. Positive meaning has intrinsic significance. This is by observation not reasoning.

Proofs are unobtainable because one only has one moment of conscious observation in the present. A chance of obtaining enough value more than an alternative certainty is worth more than that certainty. Sometimes chances become certainties. Observing the atomic is observing oneself observing the atomic which is not conscious to one. The atomic itself is not intrinsically nothing but has an alternative to consciousness. The atomic is neutral, incapable of good and bad except as we use it, and are affected. The atomic is not our things made of microscopically small parts but a separate existence. It is acceptable to paradise. The aliens have allowed is to do what we want with it because it is neutral. The aliens are mediums not bodies with different from our experience. The atomic is a giant medium. Emotion is more than one medium. People often have a different emotional medium. This will add to variety in paradise. The aliens believe our real selves should be satisfied.

Death is an end of personal good not an evil. It is a loss of positive not a negative. Consciousness continues but in other people.

Joy is a value. Joy has the description, no maximum number of steps. Further than value and further than joy. It also has no maximum further than no maximum. Want satisfying pleasure also does it. Further than answering or further than the ultimate is more likely in a positive direction than negative and the subjects gain by intrinsic positiveness. Infinite time could give better finites during all of the infinite time, giving a better infinite. Significance can be good or bad significance. Quality and pleasure are more than significant. Positiveness is wonderful in meaning and goes beyond meaning. These require unfound concepts and existence.

Have making, not war. Create negligible degrees of danger. Try to get an acceptable method for choosing the best opinion.

Aesthetics have become too wide, all that is needed are the synonyms of beauty, to add to beauty, this includes parts of goodness and quality and added is an infinite number of further steps at any finite frequency in an infinite description.

An infinite description would have an infinite number of differentiating infinites. Each one would start from a different finite position.

If bad progresses it becomes good. If it does opposite of progress it goes against itself. It if does neither is gets nowhere. This means positiveness has a greater description, which infinite bad doesn't cancel out. The positive finites composing infinity are greater.

Note book 5

Paradise has more height of truth and is more alive. It's want satisfaction is freedom. The mind has its salvation. Don't progress by raising bads, still outside paradise, avoid bads. Progress into this, into height which is rich in good or do the narrower essence of height to be within.

The future of non-paradise couldn't have the ability to master properly all the potential powers of mind it gets. If it is based on knowledge and not the best knowledge it will be wrong.

Would be bads shouldn't be bad. In non-paradise fiction they are often bad, though less bad than reality.

The word infinity can be a small infinity, while its significance is the big one. The description of a thing has a chance of infinity, the chance being negligibly against. This description is made up of finites which have infinite description and these in turn have finites with infinite descriptions, and so on. This means the descriptions are both finites and infinites.

In paradise further is based and thought of in positiveness and its direction. The earth will rise and the new Jerusalem will become on high. There are beautiful well energies. Positive quantities are more natural than negative quantities and quality and its synonyms are naturally better than their opposites. The light is life. Ultimates are probably advantages, or further in that direction. So limiting progress to that will probably produce the most ultimates, or progress goes further than just searching through knowledge. Just searching through knowledge does not include progress as this just increases good or follows answers. If opposite of progress occurs it could be temporary. There is a chance of ultimates an infinite number of steps beyond infinity.

Beauty has good truth, adorned truths and can be a consideration for belief.

Bad as a synonym of wrong is half wrong. That it rarely produces enough good makes it nearly always wrong. Paradise being the highest good makes bad wrong. Proper positiveness gives emotional and spiritual well-being.

Gain has substance. Parent friendship has good love discerning what is best and keeping to the best and the chance of unfound concepts sufficiently further than best. Perfection has a very small chance. It goes so far, in conception. So it is well done as a subject, instead, and possibly further than perfection. Perfection plus imperfection is better than just perfection. One cannot repeat perfection or that would be better. It would not differentiate. The chance of perfection in infinity is negligibly against infinity so it is as if certain. It is the same with no maximum further than infinity. This is its worth. As a truth of perfection it is still a chance. Practical perfection can be distinguished from chance of perfection.

Imagination has the reality of its phenomena, mental and descriptive, and is part of biography, and can do 'would bees'. The mind knows more than our atomic knowing. The brains semi permutations have an enormous quantity. The brain structure, without taking the semi permutations into account, is too complex for the genetic amount to give it inheritance. And, survival of the best at surviving only helped progress, during the millions of years I believe.

The worth of a thing is not the only point but what the thing is that has the worth. The reasons for the worths are what counts. Positive meaning on its own misses things.

The economics of value and the value of economics are the same thing.

Knowledge of the mind is mostly about wrongs, since the best is a lesser part, until progress creates more right than wrong, or the want of right avoids it. Leave and end wrongs except opinion of right, which must sometimes be wrong.

Don't defy mental nature heighten mental nature. Because chances of infinity could not be observed as certain the chance of infinity being negligibly against so that it is as if certain was taken to be only chance. If it is just chance it is still extremely valuable. The average finite is an infinity.

It is said 'love is blind'. Height has more wisdom. Naturalness is gentler. Add love, wisdom, naturalness, and positiveness together. Slight love is still worthwhile. Appreciation adds good. If the person you love is worth appreciating appreciation and love are better than love. Goodness and love are better than love, and conceiving further. Love, like anything, includes the whole description of nature because it is in nature, but nature is loved because love exists. Bad nature is not loved by paradise or perhaps resists good, paradise gives it.

Have the best of the past and present for the future. To heighten the world further more money in the better off countries barely helps. Heightening knowledge is needed. Suggestions from a good history of pleasure is one such subject. Also higher minorities and value in society. The psychology of satisfying pleasure. Art and society and positive effects from surroundings and other relevant subjects. Wisdom and religion is another.

Good is better than bad since it has gain and bad has loss. Good has the advantages. Bad must have partial good to have advantages. Good gives gain, bad loss. There are synonyms of good, better than synonyms of bad.

Extra page

The less bad the more cause and effect from bad in between bads and so more good from the bad. Bad causing good is often believed good, because good enough in opinion. More advanced natures may tend to non-paradise because they have so much that new things take too long to get a good fit instead of more new things so this bad may increase progress. The subject 'an infinite number of further steps than good progress is better in good than in good and bad and so this is just good.

Considerations in favour of good are in favour of just good. Good is more truly just good than good with bad.

Kinds of good have the description of all of good. Good and bad causes have all the description of good and bad.

Bad should become uncommon.

Note book 6

Infinite good and infinite bad don't meet, so infinite bad cannot have anything to do with infinite goods. We don't know full infinity, intrinsically.

Would be bads give a fuller expression than bad.

Paradise includes the magnificent.

All answers are either limitations of non-paradise . A limitation may give more scope, by better progress. The only other answer is nothing, death. The best, and quality and religion go to paradise, together. Bad for good is called good. This bad must end or almost. It is better to avoid bad than know it to end it. Avoiding bad tends to end it. Bad to cause good does not cause enough good. At present morals appear to require some bad. Pleasure is the most intrinsically positive good and positive meaning is what distinguishes from negative meaning. Pleasure being an intrinsic good has intrinsic advantages because good has advantages.

Everything has all good and bad in description but it may not always be appropriate. The ultimate has the appropriate description of all good.

Have the best good in paradise and further.

God is largely beyond imaginings ability but also limited. Knowing God is to know a representation only. God knows us in such a way that to him we are in paradise.

There are other ways of dividing us up than paradise and non-paradise. Excellence and non-excellence is one.

Morals are a treasure in paradise.

To us the atomic is in the mind and this is sacred. Live soft not hard, or live neutral. Connect with the natural, heartfelt, deeper inner self.

The body does not need to be felt bad. Death in paradise is an ending of personal good not a giving of bad.

Pleasure need not increase want without satisfaction. Enlightenment is in pleasure, and satisfaction. Reality is not the point but limited quality.

There are differences that are placed in difference not in space.

The self should only be free in that it is free to limit itself of not to attempting paradise or staying in paradise.

The heart is capable of a higher understanding.

The realist self is that which gets the best fit of experience. This is the best self for paradise. Purpose arrives at good and pleasure. Thought describes and helps organise pleasure. Not much of feeling is expressible.

Paradise by height, accumulating nicenesses that cause niceness having want satisfaction. Formulas, appreciation, quality better than just happiness and not doing bads. Further than just good. Religion helps, or can do it.

One only needs a little against bad, to be against bad but one can have any amount in favour of good.

Love and appreciation of good give good more meaning. This is the point of love.

Ones mind is a world. Ones mind is a kingdom.

Just good and its synonyms is a utopia.

Differentiating infinites have to exist as well as an infinity so they add up to more than infinity. Infinities added together are said to equal infinity.

An infinity that is always ahead of another infinity is a larger infinity because an infinity is always finite throughout infinity. So there is no need to add infinity to infinity, to get infinity. Finite improvement of infinity becomes possible. A step better maintained to infinity is an infinite number of steps further. Paradise is the best choice. Paradise is an ideal. Infinitely better than paradise is a subject paradise does. The subject makes it partly there by aspects of its nature.

Love gives meaning to good. Meaning has significance. Significance and point have meaning. A little meaning is a great infinite, with infinite hidden meaning because of a chance of an infinite description which is the same as the thing described. A little meaning is better than an infinity without meaning or have an alternative to meaning.

The chance of infinity is negligibly against compared to infinity so it is as if certain.

Nature has quality because it has understanding. It is understandable so that is probably where the answer to what to do with life occurs. Most likely in quality and its synonyms. There is a chance and subject of an endless number of answers. It makes no difference to the quantity, if infinite, whether they are found quickly or slowly so more scope is not needed for this most important aim. Several aims at once are possible. Nature works like the understanding. It is reasonable, for example, that red and blue make purple. Wrong is not reasonable but works in an understandable way.

Lessen bad until there's hardly any.

The brain has so many combinations that the newer parts of the brain haven't had enough time to integrate well with so much. This is in favour of quicker progress needing bads. There is a proper bias in unfound knowledge in favour of good since good has the advantages. Bad has none except with good or being partly good.

Infinity goes so far that this subject is better than an ultimate in unfound concepts. The advantages belong more truly to good not good with bad. This means in unfound knowledge good with bad tends to be cut down although it gets more.

Goodness brings more life. Paradises life glory and nature is insistently and consistently available lifting and gladdening with constant blessings. From yourself and others.

Love is wasted if upon someone who cannot be made more good than he otherwise would be.

Aesthetics can include anything in a high reason or high form. This has positive meaning. Beauty and its synonyms. Being has both negative and positive meaning and neutrality.

The new way superseded positive meaning.

If answering will sooner or later answer good with good and bad just good will sooner or later answer that.

The answer is emphasisable. If there are an infinite number of answers paradise has a finite fraction of this which is still infinite. The same is true of more scope, less scope has a finite fraction of infinite answering which is infinites. Finite is negligible, as infinitely small compared to infinity. Aesthetics should not say what art is but what it should be. Quality is an advantage to art, and its synonyms. So much so it cannot do without it. Paradise has quality and its synonyms in pleasure. Aesthetics should be good and the good moral, and infinitely further than good, in a good direction.

The good as the possible or subject of the beginning after nothing of a direction can be conceived as having an infinite number of answering steps. The chance of this is negligibly against compared to infinity. So it is equivalent to infinite.

If good has an infinitely small fraction of infinite answering then it has a finite number of answers expect that the average finite is infinite. Or because there are an infinite number of infinites in an infinity an infinitely small fraction is infinite answering.

The description of anything is the same as the thing described so it is there.

Creation follows positive number increase because negative numbers go towards nothing not to the opposite of the creation. Value is one of these positive number increases. The creation grows because positive and negative numbers stretch to infinity. Meaning emphasises the positive. Increase is obviously positive. Value increases partly because the creation increases in various ways. One complete nothing is something and there is nothing so there is two completed nothings and a nothing and is on to infinity. Nature begins because nothing has a description and gives size to an infinity of positive numbers. In emotion meaning comes from its richness. This richness is in all emotion. Intrinsically richness has an emphasis in quantity. Richness is more appropriate to treasure than negativeness. The creation is a treasure. Progress increases positiveness unless this is answered.

Aim at a most good best quality paradise. Our deep self is worth connecting to pleasure.

Infinite time is always finite but the subject infinity or no maximum avoids this. The subject infinite answering and no maximum answering in a quality direction is improved upon by the subject quality and its synonyms. This includes no maximum answering, and all quality is infinite due to the chance of infinite description. Also all quality has as if no maximum value, due to the chance of no maximum description.

The chance is negligibly against compared to infinity and no maximum. Quality includes all answers to quality in its appropriate description. The subject infinitely further than quality in a quality direction is better than any finite answer because a finite answer cannot be infinitely certain and the chance of infinitely further is better. The subject makes its thing partly there by aspects of its nature. But not knowing what quality will turn up means quality and its synonyms is the best subject.

Infinity is not just always going further but complete as always there. It has an infinite number of finites. An infinite number of steps beyond quality gives better and better infinites, because the natures are each throughout infinity. Possibly a no maximums number of steps beyond quality is the true holiness.

Christ believed in good and bad.

Progress and intention will soon produce more paradise. Some people are in paradise. Paradise is quality and its synonyms in pleasure with want satisfaction, and the subject a no maximum number of further steps, which makes itself partly real by aspects of its nature, and is possibly still paradise.

Paradise could do it at a fraction of no maximum being no maximum.

The object of the instrumental is the intrinsic. One can want the intrinsic in the first place. The intrinsic tends to be instrumental and is chosen for intrinsic quality, and its pleasure. The point of the instrumental is the intrinsic.

Infinitely further can be one step in an infinite number of steps passing infinity. Better than an answer is the subject endless answering, which makes itself partly real by aspects of its nature. The answers tend to contribute to nature. The total value is the main value not the best. Progressing to a better part of infinity before following an answer will not improve infinity. Following the different answers differentiates between them. Knowledge has an infinite number of steps better than the truth and this is partly real by aspects of its nature. But this is just one answer.

The appropriate description of pleasure is pleasure.

Anything has a chance, negligible compared to infinity, of the description of the ultimate in an infinite description, so it is an ultimate. Good does it better than bad. The description is the same as the thing described so it as if there.

Infinity, if it exists has no end to finiteness.

Paradise has advantages in proper pleasure. If you would be truly blessed believe in God and find his ways for your heart.

There are three answers to the sum an infinitely small fraction of infinity. One, infinity because there are an infinite number of infinites in an infinite, and any finite which averages at infinity. The average of these three is infinity. So the chance of infinite or other infinite could be infinitely small.

A different infinite gives a further presence so it is not infinite plus infinite equals infinite.

Lessen and avoid intrinsic bad. If not intrinsic descriptive bad is made intrinsic and got rid of, it will still be in the same description beyond the intrinsic.

Selection is by going to paradise. Sins are not prohibitive, because paradise is an improvement and punishment is not believed in by paradise. The world is half way to heaven.

The real self has a potential nobleness and an inner greatness and is capable of contributing well to the world.

We need a new bible just concerned with good and further than good, without bad. If you are much of a maker in the mind you can make paradise in yourself.

Having to have more than exceptional bad is more dangerous.

Answers in finite time cannot be infinitely certain so a chance of infinitely further answering is better. Paradise at a fraction of the infinity that good and bad may do is still infinite answering: the same size. The answers are to the question, what to do? The subject 'infinitely past pleasure' is past pleasure, but best done in pleasure, unless a better intrinsic is found.

Each thing has a chance of an infinite description. This emphasises the difference between good and bad. Good in pleasure has a double advantage, or two sets of advantages.

Our brains could be chemically similar to animals brains for more good. Perhaps the hormones are different. Knowledge is mostly wrongs and neutrals not the best.

Since infinity is entirely made up of finites the average value of all the finites counts and can vary giving infinites of different values. If it reaches infinite value at infinity the finites can still be larger or smaller during all the infinity, giving different value infinites. The finites are without end but in a way infinity never reaches infinity as it is always finite, being composed of finites. The finites are always there so it is complete to be infinite.

If we are not always justified we are forgiven but it is better to be justified. Forgiveness for the sake of paradise, that does not go in for punishment and does not believe in bad. The morals of non-paradise include bads. Less good does not have to be defined as including bads but more good is preferable. The morals of paradise are easy because they have to be nice and completely wanted, though will power can be used, for less good for more good, when there's a gain. Freedom may mean this is not essential. Freedom adds value to the less valuable, justifying it. Freedom also adds value to the more valuable if done but this is not always achieved by freedom. There is a chance of an infinitely more acceptable description that just morals. The description of nature includes the description of morals since one can say in describing "further things are" and give the rest of nature. Would be bads are done instead of bads. Each bad has more than one would be bad. The immoral is not appropriate description. The description of nature is in morals because the description is the same thing as the thing described.

Paradise is taken as the same size as good and bad. A fraction of infinity which is infinite.

A fraction of no maximum from the chance of no maximum equals no maximum. A fraction of infinitely past infinity from the chance of infinitely past infinity equals infinitely past infinity. Infinite plus finite does not have as good a chance as infinitely further than infinity, and finite plus infinitely past infinity does not have as good a chance as no maximum. Just finite doesn't have a good enough chance. Paradise may be a fraction of the size of doing anything and anything has a chance of infinity, etc. so does paradise. Further than a concept in its direction includes the finite and the infinite and no maximum and so is better.

Doing good had a chance of an infinite description including a positive ultimate. The bad ultimate has no advantages and the full form doesn't come from progress. The full form of description comes in infinite time unless the infinite leaves out some. No maximum is possible and is a subject. Good has a greater description in infinity due to progress and its potential than bad. This means it has greater finites. If bad has any advantages it is because it is being partly good or with good. One doesn't need to observe an infinity in the evaluation or alternative to evaluation. Good has the advantages so makes a better ultimate than bad. Bad and good both at infinity is greater in good.

The atomic need not be felt when one is awake. Only the mind need be felt. There is no proof of the atomic existing as the so called proof may be only mind things possibly with causes in the unconscious. Nature organises because cause and effect are understandable, and because number is partly organised. The understandable is slightly touched with positive meaning in the otherwise plain atomic to itself. High organisation and high meaning is caused in paradise and possibly fuller meaning. Positive and not negative meaning is true and real meaning. The first cause may be part of the description of nothing. This makes it something, and has potential meaning. The subject further than positive meaning is a possibility.

Infinitely further gives a better chance than a finite, though a smaller chance.

The truth of good and such is a way of knowing God. The description of nothing exists because a description is the same as the thing described. It doesn't need the full description to add up to the thing described, and a description of nothing could have started the universe.

If considerations are in favour of good because it has the advantages and just bad has none than the considerations are in favour of just good. Just good only has advantages. Good and bad has advantages and disadvantages. In all cases more so and not in the same proportion as the considerations already known. Unknown degrees of good and bad comparable with just intrinsic good.

It is not natural for infinite or no maximum bads to meet infinite or no maximum goods. The difference is too great.

There are many considerations to take from other schools of morals than the one.

Morals are in thought and feeling, feeling gives life. Thought can be in feeling. Thought includes the reason. Chance in thought is enough for morals. The self is consciousness a medium and character. Ones self and other selves are loved in Christianity. The truth liberates, it can cause paradise.

Assessing and attraction are two forms of evaluation. The specialist needs the details of description.

There are positive feelings which improve feelings.

Be natural and relaxed.

The description of a no maximum number of steps past pleasure in the direction of pleasure can be in the description of pleasure. A fraction of no maximum is no maximum. But, a better no maximum is got by better during it. The about reality of aspects of its nature. A description can add up to a thing described without full description and without full reality. Further steps take it constantly better or beyond better in a better direction, or at suitable angles.

The subject is done in pleasure for more value. Its chance of reality is negligibly against compared to no maximum and so it evaluates as if certain. The subject can assume one goes past the ultimate and pleasure in unfound concepts, or phenomena.

At any rareness a no maximum number of concepts of any sort is likely to exist in a no maximum description.

Pleasure heightens other values and is the most important intrinsic known. Further than pleasure is not known intrinsically.

Constant pleasure with want satisfaction is more valuable than pleasure and nastiness with not want and satisfaction on non-paradise.

Best wishes from me for you all.

Note book 7

Paradise is an answer divine. Pleasure is all because would bees take the place of nastiness. Love is better. Excellence flourishes. Quality is height. Infinity and no maximum are everywhere. All is superseded. Meaning has strength, and direction. Paradise can also be a utopia, and high good. Good gives more and better chances of beyond, than bad, partly by better progress. Just anything doesn't have the additional chance. Freedom economy and sensibleness are proper. Slight improvements by the ton can be very good. Wider than economics is needed. Harmony and love are good together. Synonyms of pleasure can be in pleasure, good and quality for example. Have an eager life. Paradise is better than non-paradise. Refinement and much good constitute it, intrinsically; tons of treasure. It is organised for more pleasure and worthwhileness. Sensibleness is a slight pleasure to increase. It exists organising.

Advantages are good and there are none in more appropriate description of bad so they are in favour of just good not also bad causing apparently enough good, because just good is the real good. Good touches eternity but evil isn't wanted by eternity. Beauty is in a relationship with divine glory. Morals and the answers for life are better with pleasure and want satisfaction. The saying 'beauty, goodness and truth go together' is well known. Pleasure has an aesthetic and a spiritual side.

There is infinite goodness. There is the subject total good truth and supreme pleasure, and further in their direction. Be properly radiant. Good advantages assist progress. Advantages are gains. Better progress could mean more scope. Beauty has higher kinds of organisation of fit, harmony, proportion and wholeness, and positiveness. Wisdom also brings better order. It also tends to reflect beauty. In knowledge infinitely further is a chance and subject. Chances of infinity are important. The chance of infinite good is better than the chance of infinite bad because good has the known advantages. Advantages and disadvantages have been all that was thought to matter during our development from the unknown and so that will most likely continue in our things. Any aliens may be different but we will still have to do our things. Things should fit us. Our unknown probably belongs to nature and to us. Do we want to be ourselves? If we don't keep our basic natures there will be a great loss, as long as they are capable of contributing greatness to nature. The aliens may integrate and they may want us in paradise. If aliens gave us so many good things to do we had no time for bad. This would be better. The future effects beforehand, as I believe does happen, a new future is created by new previous cause and effect. This future can be not yet there, and there is no need to repeat the past future with its wrong.

Perfection with eternity with the ultimate and the absolute good is better than just the ultimate. The advantages of paradise will help good and answering go beyond good and answering, as will more scope by progress. One can probably serve aspects of the subject "infinitely better than progress". Infinity is completed in finites because it is composed of finites. If there is infinite we have begun it. Better finites during infinity means better differentiating infinites during infinity by a chance of an infinite description of the finite, the chance being negligible. Knowledge can be limited for the sake of advantages and progress since they may have an infinite description.

Every bad would be good might would do better as a good while other bads have good would be bads more than the quantity of bads. Pleasure is intrinsically a more positive good. Emotion is rich. Richness is closer to treasure than opposite of treasure and so one may expect more pleasure than nastiness potentially but wrongs are potentially more than right because the best is only one opinion yet one needs to allow other opinions of what is right. This causes wrongs in paradise but alternatives with nastiness in them are not included only more and less good, intrinsically, to the observation. This has other debateable good. Majorities are not always right and the best opinion according to the nature of judgement is not yet a certain science. Alternatively one goes ones own way.

Christ emphasising holy men and morals misses the points that are happiness, pleasure and want satisfaction and well-being. A plain experience has a large paradise description. Sensory vision and sound are plain. Dimensional scent will heighten vision. Memory improved. Genius commonplace. Psychological making to satisfy the individual being made. Keeping high, wonderful treasure, emotional gold. Enhancements. Wonders. Being more happy, if you were happy. Right, in good opinion. Godliness. Style when wanted. The holistic way of life. Friendliness. Automation of unwanted work. A good home. Christ lifting. More than words can say. Angelic help, if available. Further adventure. Economics. Niceness within niceness. Historical high insights. High insights from autobiography. History of the arts (mostly). Physics, biology and chemistry, without bad. Social welfare. Efficiency: autocratic height. Employment with pleasure. Steps to achievement and height beyond the normal limit.

Nature as we know it and our own nature should fit for health. The order of the universe is akin to music. Wisdom and not foolishness takes precedence in nature. Wisdom is in favour of beauty, and orders beautifully, in good, when enough applied, and organises beauty properly. Positiveness is more reasonable than negativeness and more desirable so nature is more positive than negative, because nature works like the understanding. This is why it can be understood. The neutralness of the atomic gives an opportunity of good or bad feeling for it with good preferred, and good helped evolution. Order is appropriate to quality. Paradise is glorious not nature, unless the animals are in paradise (with pain an exception.) Appreciation helps heighten. Organising gives an opportunity of more good. Opposite of progress gets nowhere and is not successful so potential progress in description makes nature valuable. Progress is more wantable and makes nature good. Anything is an ultimate because anything has a chance of an infinite description with an infinite ultimate described in it and the chance gets less and less significant into infinity. So good things are good ultimates. This is in favour of them. An infinite description could be part of an infinite description, giving more value than the ultimate. Although all nature is in the description of good and the ultimate the more appropriate counts more. One can say when describing 'other things are' and refer to the rest of nature. The more appropriate description of good is just good. Paradise has the highest good. Pleasure adds to the value of good. Its attractiveness shows value. This value describes to infinity. Pleasure adds to good. Its attractiveness shows good. It also shows worthwhileness. Pleasure is infinitely good due to its chance of an infinite description in good, good being more appropriate.

At a proportion of infinite good there can be a description in infinite pleasure, composed of differentiating infinites which add to more than infinity. The descriptions are there because they are the same as the things described, although the things described have finite intrinsics. They also have a possible infinite potential of cause and effect. In paradise pleasure keeps causing pleasure. Bad doesn't cause enough good to justify some. Progress may more or less end intentional bad, bad tending to end for increasing good. Half good half bad is wrong. Pleasure includes various intrinsic more valuable qualities than just good, or so I believe. The infinites add their finites during infinity together to greater finites during infinity. Nature is glorious to paradise.

Bad is not a form of good but its opposite. Related but opposite. Do your ideal in paradise for further point. Paradise beauty is very desirable. Religion is heightened. The weather feels fine whatever it does. If there is a God he feels all in paradise. Dirt is just less good, not bad. The arts are just quality, bad in the arts isn't wanted and bad is often higher than in reality in the arts. Death is the end of some good not the doing of bad. No need for negative experience. Consciousness will continue in other people, perhaps yourself. During disease there is only pleasure, and want satisfaction. Bad is known without bad by would be bads. Simultations, formulas, heightenings and blends are examples, all in pleasure, blends are blended with enough pleasure to be nice. One should not find bad to make would bees out of it. The aesthetic, moral, and spiritual can go together.

The brain could be the source of much knowledge.

Absolute beauty is in a possible God. Infinites in infinity, the chances being negligible. Infinitely better than beauty if a God can do it, is possible. Infinitely past infinity and always better is a subject. Is there a God who can really do anything? Perhaps to do the most God is still creating himself and progressing into infinity. All of nature is in the description of each thing. A finite nature would be infinitely less than an infinite God. This is in favour of the chance of infinite nature. Christ beloved in punishment. Paradise does not believe in punishment because of its nastiness. The cross should be rare. The possible God is in paradise or what it becomes better or a preferable alternative to better. Pleasure is slight compared to its possible infinity of description and cause and effect, but meaning is a most fortunate occurrence, and pleasure has meaning. Meaning may not be conceived without meaning. It comes from richness and richness possibly comes from the potential of plain. God or nature, or both possibly come from a description of nothing which being the same thing as the thing described existed as well as nothing. Just nothing was impossible.

Just pleasure cuts down opinion. Reality is the truth but the truth is largely wrongs.

The best opinion is perhaps got by applying and collecting knowledge of judgement quality. Reality is nice, nasty and neutral. Neutral at the same time in the person as pleasure is possible acceptable to paradise.

Paradise is not limited to the pleasure and want satisfaction but to its wider language, and what it means. For example the subject certain infinitely better than paradise which makes it partly real by aspects of its nature. Going further than pleasure or whatever is you cannot say what because whatever you say it could be something else unknown at present. The chance or subject of infinity here is not the answer but an unknown entity. The chance or subject is done in paradise for more value, adding to the contribution to nature.

Anything is an ultimate but the negative ultimate may not be made worthwhile by this, because the negative has the disadvantages. So the positive ultimate is better. Paradise is an ultimate with known advantages. Positiveness is gain. The chance of an infinite ultimate is negligible compared to infinity. Paradise has such a chance in its description, the description being the same as the thing described, and infinite with the infinite ultimate in it. Eternal paradise is an answer but infinitely further than pleasure and want satisfaction can be done as a subject in paradise, and service of aspects of the subject. An infinite number of further steps is conceived but no maximum goes further than infinity, and gives a better answer.

Morals should bring happiness or paradise. We shouldn't do bad to cause good. Pleasant creativity and use of thought can develop morals and spirit with enthusiasm. The morals of paradise are nice and wanted, not needing willpower, or not much. Less nice but still nice for sufficiently more nice, less meaning for sufficiently more meaning; and there whether in oneself or others. Perhaps this less is not often better. Morals should bring comfort and joy. The child in a good home gets a good disposition and this helps morals. Take proper pleasure. Nobleness helps happiness. Governing oneself should be natural. Be right within your heart. Progress in pleasure. Mankind has a spiritual nature. Wisdom, beauty and goodness go together. Faith, moral pleasure and love go together so that one does not love nastiness.

If you keep being positive this means all is well. Using strengths and emotions positively increases happiness. Quality and proper pleasure has the synonyms of quality; point, worthwhileness, good, advantages, value, gain and positiveness. In spiritual joy is meaning that supports faith. Quality should be more and instead of bad. Proper pleasure has intrinsic quality which gives it meaning. Sometimes it has further meaning as well. Best quality includes less value to add to more total value. The best average is not needed but the best average times the number of cases, which is the total value. Efficiency is helpful. Excellence an aim. During infinity is always finite so better finites during infinity would mean a better infinity. Spending more time on each thing gives better finites and slow progress. The chance of infinite time makes this worthwhile. Twice the value of infinites gives twice the value of the infinite. Some things the same can feel better and some new better things can be found, with improved feeling as well. Wisdom can increase pleasure. Paradise is more in keeping with the truth and is more alive. Its want satisfaction is the best.

Fit the person. Be relaxed. The Garden of Eden is still half there. The brain is not well appropriate to the environment since we are hardly concerned with complex brain effects, and their evaluation. Spiritual transcendency tends towards the infinite and ecstasy, which are in its higher self. Christ to be holy does not believe in punishment. Paradise does not believe in nastiness and God is the main paradise possibility. Anyone is welcome to paradise should they keep its nature, otherwise they are not in paradise while they do different. Freedom is justified in adding value to the less valuable and the more valuable but the less valuable gets more valuable than the more valuable alternative without freedom so although it is not the most valuable choice it is better. So one doesn't leave paradise by doing the less valuable in freedom and want satisfaction. Then is alright, in that respect.

The chance of no maximum good and furthest in that direction is a larger chance than the opposite for bad or non –paradise, because good and not bad has known progress and good has the advantages not known bad. Pleasure or good gets more from beyond which improves its chances because it has more to create with.

The universe is much more than infinitely valuable, and we can make it better. This by greater finites and better chance, and differentiating infinites. We can also join in the good. Greater finites tending throughout the no maximum improves it, but attempting quick progress may make too many mistakes, and would miss lesser contributions and would miss some major contributions. It takes time to make knowledge good enough. Most alternatives are wrongs. Niceness and want satisfaction are already as answer; other answers and problems come within these two. Nature has the subject no maximum further than the best, in the best direction. If infinity exists the finite is always present. Nature may have an infinite number of differentiating infinites and this just another differentiating infinite among others, never ending at an infinity, and it is not that infinity is without end. There is also a chance of infinitely further than infinity existing and differentiating and allowing further.

This is largely mystery, but a subject. Subjects make themselves partly real by aspects of their subjects nature. There is the subject grace extending to no maximum. Concepts or references at any finite or infinite rareness in a no maximum description give a no maximum number of concepts in a good direction if arranged in order of most or further.

True repetition doesn't differentiate so would bring history to an end, so constant difference throughout infinity is needed.

Bad cannot cause enough good. Good goes to height. Paradise is then chosen for more meaning. Treasure want satisfaction and intrinsic quality and other heights, of

123

mind and spirit. The arts are heightened further and life always higher.

Good or paradise has a chance of a description giving an infinite number of steps further than infinite value. The chance is negligible compared to infinity. Good has better chances in the unknown than doing anything in knowledge. A finite part of an infinite description has an infinite description. The incomplete subject good or likewise paradise has a chance of a description giving an infinite number of steps further than infinite value. The ideal is only one alternative. Most of the answer lies in other things: adding to more value or an alternative to value. Everything belongs to existence so that is where the answer to life is.

Bad but bad cannot cause enough good because it does not have the right meaning. In favour of good is mostly in favour of just good or this is the real good. The other is good requiring bad. Good in unfound considerations doesn't have to justify bad. This gives a proper bias. The good apparently caused by some bad is used to justify when any alternative just good appears not to be enough.

Paradise can do the subject of an infinite number of steps beyond paradise. This may be in the description of paradise at any rareness or not of concept and other references. The subject makes its self partly real by aspects of its nature. The references make better and better infinites during infinity, which is always finite. The infinites also differentiate.

The absolute is possible religious, and might be superseded by unknown references, or concepts. The chance of a no maximum number of steps beyond the absolute, possibly in its direction is better than a finite quantity of references found, but both are possible.

The absolute may be infinite apart from an infinite description as also may eternity. No maximum goes further than infinity. A description of nothing which existed in the beginning of things because a description is the same as the thing described may have created God in infiniteness. One complete nothing and nothing not counted gives two complete nothings and nothing not counted and this gives three and so on to infinity. This could have started things, or helped to. Quantity to exist may take the form of other reality and so everything could be quantity, or nearly. Nothing can be said not to have the number one but to say one does not exist gives it existence in the saying of it. Not one nothing becomes one nothing. At any rate, can nothing exist without some description? Religion can give heaves on earth, a heaven of joy and comfort, with a crown. By a knowledge and life of faith with assurance, blessed and in grace and happiness. The crown comes from grace and Christ: where you become a son or daughter of apparent God. Assurance comes from certain evident knowledge that you have grace and that you have faith. Christian heaven on earth can also be in a manmade paradise. We can chose between paradise and non-paradise for the future. I believe God will support a man-made paradise.

Infinite time is either best served by slow progress with more development or quicker progress than that which is always finitely ahead of what is would have been but still goes to infinity. Slow progress puts more development into infinity using more time with each answer that comes, not perfect as they are.

 The chance of infinite time matters, not a finite time strictly speaking chances are not negligible compared to infinity but compared to infinite value or alternative to value being infinite. Everything is at least one step. The greater the difference in quantity between good and bad during infinite time the better the infinite, if the most is the goodness. During infinite time is different from complete infinity. During infinite time, time is always finite. Infinity is composed of finites. During infinity is a form of infinity. So if nature is no maximum greater good than bad each one of us can make a difference adding good or pleasure. The better infinite keeps its better point with other infinites, even an infinite number of infinites. The proportion will work instead. A better proportion during infinity giving better infinity. One can take an infinite number if steps past anything, in subject.

Christians are asked to do on earth as in heaven. A paradise is part of that. Right is assisted by ability and proper wealth applied. Righteousness is not glory, at the best righteousness. Right improves glory and includes glory. Paradise can contain a range of moral opinions all limited within niceness satisfying want. Values are not enough without morals. Values do not always help quality enough. Christianity cannot do without power. Grace heightens morals. There is freedom, Christ and God helping, forgiveness, love providing incentive, and motive, beauty of religious and high moral feeling. The spirit of loveliness has it, and positiveness and eternity in feeling. One shouldn't love good and bad. Each of these things has a chance of an infinite description. Be pure and natural in heart. Have pleasure in peace. Spiritual right is better than just morals. The cross is wrong in bad. It is the internal that matters about the external, and other internal life. The material world can be felt in spirit, or mind.

Finites during infinity have chances of infinite descriptions. Finites during infinity may cause infinities in infinite time. Finites may cause infinite in God's eternity if there is one. Finites may also cause no maximums.

The spiritual is better than the material except perhaps many peoples material benefit compared to the spiritually personal. Undifferentiating infinites add up to one infinity except somewhat if they are with new associations. Good and good with bad both have infinity with a negligible chance against as the truth.

Greatness adds to other things. The quantity of good gives its distance from bad which has depth of significance. Pleasure can add its good to good by having good in pleasure. This is a further heightening of good. Positiveness can also add to quality of meaning and heighten the spiritual. Qualities can have quality meaning. If all good is quality, this gives more point, if the two are distinguishable. Pleasure heightens quality and good, adding various quantities of positiveness. This is magnified by possible infinite description. A small pleasure can be about many people. Paradise goes further than happiness in intrinsic quality. Evaluation gives selection of the best, but the best is improved upon by the subject an infinite number of steps past the best. The subject gains partial reality by aspects of the subject. Each step is a differentiating infinite, by possible infinite descriptions. The possibilities being negligibly against compared to infinity.

Aesthetics should be about quality and its synonyms. This means beauty and its synonyms, because beauty is a synonym of quality and the synonyms are synonyms of each other. Everything, that is, each thing, is either positive, negative or neutral, and so good and its synonyms are wide enough for aesthetics. This is the same thing. Good is a synonym of quality and the synonyms are synonyms of each other. Proper pleasure and want satisfaction are the best good to do my great subjects in, for added value and add holiness. One can conceive of an infinite number of steps part anything, and a no maximum. Good in aesthetics includes as it is done in the arts: beauty, holiness, appreciation, pleasure, want satisfaction, quality, and the nature of happiness. For example, social welfare or good personal character are only slightly aesthetic, perhaps more so in paradise, but good and its synonyms contain all worthwhile aesthetics.

Beauty heightens in various ways so usefulness probably increases, being there without intention or especially for it.

That which to give attention to has a best choice. Alternatives have a best choice. Comparison comes into it. Chances come into it. Values come into it. Build upon. Attitude should be good. Everyday life should be enchanting. One should not be in disharmony. This means being harmoniousness or neutral. In general don't resist pleasures. Sensual pleasures have advantage, of health and ability. Rightness, enjoyment, enthusiasm and energy go together. Good and its synonyms are more important than just the aesthetics of them "having a good time" means a time of happiness, or intrinsic quality, in the world of good and bad. Then real self is not being made unnatural. Being unnatural is unpleasant. You can become an angel with your own version of worthwhile knowledge, applied. Fantastic subjects can be made partly real by aspects of their nature, more ways to paradise can be found, without being fantastic. Tantric is a path of ecstasy. Books on how to do enjoyment, pleasure, joy or bliss exist. Happiness can be improved upon. Books heightening work exist. Books on quality can be applied to paradise. The pleasure of former high society could be applied. Good made into pleasure. Selections made. Revolution for those who want it. A paradise of harmony attempted. Money can be applied for research or thought. To limited can be expanded. Television made beautiful would not need so much choice with a larger three dimensional image. Better progress from better good giving more scope later possibly than good and bad. Evaluation should heighten. Sanctuary can have added pleasure. Recreation and leisure kept. Flower gardens improved. Flourishing made into pleasure. Wonders of eternity.

Paradise can be added. It could come from afar or the south sea islands . A pole could help cause it. The artist William Morris conceived of an earthly paradise. One can add pure pull. The holy has Christ's crown. A gate could open on to it and a gate embellish it. A wreath heightens it. An end to nasty wrongs could be. The poor will go high. High mountains. New see land. So women lie to the maker. Freedom to speak out in democracy. It can be a harvest. Dancing high answering with music. Creative nip on. Including far. Could have a pure king. An end to the fishy. Christ on the cross heightened. Women winning. War no more. Gold on, no selfishness. Christmas. Finland say ran. Do my in car. Just ideas or causing action. Tribal paradise. Ending wrongs you gain. The rose using, enlarged. Aid of ease. The flying doctor service. Things planned by husband and wife. High culture. Trying to add. Slight sue except blended to avoid. Mild low. Good seed. Dove of peace. Lotus blossoms. Love with roses. Flowers in height. Recent pleasures.

It is enough if paradise can progress well enough. Specialising in knowledge is an alternative and development rather than progress is relevant to it.

Progress in pleasure could perhaps go beyond pleasure by using the language and description of pleasure which goes beyond the word pleasure in pleasure. Would be bads extend the range fully, as far as is known.

Pleasure and knowledge both can make use of scope within a maximum of infinity or no maximum. Paradise new knowledge has the addition of pleasure compared to knowledge from anything and could go just as far perhaps further into the unknown, without the range, but more in its limited range, due to progress being better with the limit. The limit being satisfying proper pleasure. Just knowledge is largely about wrongs as right as proper satisfying pleasure, is only one alternative.

None paradise appears to be wrongs, unless the knowledge changes to in favour. It may apparently keep changing between the two but good stays positive, and pleasure desirable, with want satisfaction, so this should help determine between the two. Paradise is positive and high.

Heaven if it exists is a paradise of angels and God, and people mostly in the afterlife. Love without love of bad is the possible key to heaven. Knowledge is good and evil and the fall of man to knowledge is incomplete. Knowledge in paradise is good. The same morals can feel more positive. Morals under love are emphasised in Christianity as a way to heaven. Just knowledge is for what it may find. The morals are done in glory in heaven.

131

Fulfilment and contentment should be created by paradise. This adds to happiness. Positive psychology can mean just pleasure and fulfilment and want satisfaction if the psychological needs can be satisfied by them.

If not, we can progress into it. If you want yourself you will want to be whole. There are those who believe personal development is to wholeness and joy, learning from good and bad. If we don't quickly progress to pleasure just good may be the answer. By pleasure and want satisfaction I mean want satisfying pleasure.

Charity generally causes bad of self-denial for good effect. But as love is possibly the way the world works, one can believe in it.

The finites that compose infinity are also infinites, intrinsically finite to observation. Better finites during infinity gives better infinites. Infinity being composed of finites is always finite except the total of, or what becomes of the finites, so infinite plus infinite equalling infinite doesn't count during infinity.

In knowing beyond we know non-paradise because paradise infrequently integrates with non-paradise. Infinity loses contact with itself being without end, so is only partly real. Good has a chance of an infinite ultimate in its description, but so does anything. This chance is negligible compared to infinity but good also may cause the finding of a better certainty of an ultimate. Bad is not so good a gamble. This applies to pleasure. The best or ultimate is not the narrow way one alternative suggests.

Paradise is more than infinitely valuable. Infinitely high in subject, glory beyond glory. This makes a better ultimate. Anything has a negligible chance of an infinite ultimate in its description, and the description is there since it adds up to the same as the thing described. The infinite is an infinite number of infinites in one. Grace is raised. Quality is more than for happiness. These make a better ultimate. Paradise is the best ultimate available. Better than best in unfound concepts or further. One cannot say in what way because whatever one says it could be something else, unknown. Perhaps an infinite number of steps better than infinite good, in description, and meaning. The word infinite can be a small infinity. Because infinity is complete it can be contained. So the statement infinitely better than infinite good can be a real infinite. The boundless just disappears out of sight whereas infinitely is all there. Infinity has no end. Paradise should be pure. It progresses to all wonderful. It enriches without needing much wealth. It is probably a constant treasure. People are always liked or loved, when in paradise, by paradise people. Paradise is more precious than gold. It is divine, though not heaven. It includes high meaning. Heaven may be found in paradise, love appreciation and heightening can make anything known to God in heaven. The infinite may go further than the ultimate and infinitely further than the infinite. Better and better or whatever. The full description of nature belongs to wrong and right. Right needs its more appropriate description. One can say in describing anything "the rest if nature is there" and that gives it a relationship with the thing described.

Tolerance instead of suffering plus other heightening can put anything into paradise. Paradise is next to heaven, but perhaps God has further than heaven, into the unknown. There is a list of things with no name including the positive, the worthwhile, the moral, eternity. The ultimate, substance, meaning, good, right, treasure, quality, etc. The unknown may add to this list, and beat all of them by a long way, beating infinitely further than infinity applied to any of them. The appropriate description is of unknown size with a chance of infinity. The best answer is that answering or whatever it becomes continues infinitely, and one serves the answers or whatever during infinity not find a find answer to then serve. So we progress and include the subject an infinite number of steps further than progress in a progress direction, since description has a negligible chance against of being infinite. Progress itself is more than infinitely valuable. There is a negligible chance against of infinitely more answering than to a final answer. Infinity is likely to more than answer.

Have grace in morals, morals in grace. Don't be firm. Semi-tolerance of moral opinion is not semi-tolerance of immortality. It is right that people have the freedom to have their own opinions.

Advantages benefit nature and make nature more desirable. If good is emphasised enough there will be next to no room for bad. Constant but varying degrees of quality are always in paradise: quality and highness.

The indefinite in quantity is infinite. If it is finite it is definitely finite. The degrees of moral good and bad are indefinite.

6681865R00077

Printed in Great Britain
by Amazon.co.uk, Ltd.,
Marston Gate.